SOMETHI[NG]
HAPPENED T[O]

* A woman who credits a miracle for the day her long-time alcoholic husband stopped drinking—forever.

* The young couple sure they will be forced to leave the home they love until the morning the wife awakens certain that a dramatic turnaround will change everything—and it does.

* The coed who doesn't make an important date—and finds the love of her dreams.

* The frustrating case of a flat tire that can't be changed—just long enough to keep a woman from a fatal traffic accident.

* The knife-wielding man at an ATM machine who meets the unexpected and is turned away from committing a desperate crime.

* A lightning strike that leaves a family safe, untouched and amazed at the peculiar "damage" left behind.

DON'T MISS THE INSPIRING
STORIES OF . . .

MIRACLES ON MAIN STREET

MIRACLES
ON
MAIN
STREET

VERONICA RAY

St. Martin's Paperbacks

Quote from *The Prophet*, by Kahlil Gibran, reprinted by permission of Alfred A. Knopf/Random House, publisher. Quotes from *The Tao of Pooh* by Benjamin Hoff. Copyright © 1982 by Benjamin Hoff. Used by permission of Dutton Signet, a division of Penguin Books USA Inc. Quote from *Creation Spirituality: Liberating Gifts for the Peoples of the Earth* by Matthew Fox. Copyright © 1991 by Matthew Fox. Reprinted by permission of HarperCollins Publishers, Inc. Quotes from *Breakfast at the Victory* by James P. Carse. Copyright © 1994 by James P. Carse. Reprinted by permission of HarperCollins Publishers, Inc. Quotes from *Healing Words* by Larry Dossey. Copyright © 1993 by Larry Dossey, M.D. Reprinted by permission of HarperCollins Publishers, Inc. Portions from "A Course in Miracles" © copyright 1975. Reprinted by permission of the Foundation for Inner Peace, Inc., P.O. Box 598, Mill Valley, CA 94942.

MIRACLES ON MAIN STREET

Copyright © 1996 by Veronica Ray.

ISBN: 0-312-95700-9

Printed in the United States of America

St. Martin's Paperbacks edition/January 1996

10 9 8 7 6 5 4 3 2 1

❦ ❦ ❦

*The highest achievement
of the spiritual life
is within the full embrace
of the ordinary.*

—James P. Carse, *Breakfast at the Victory*

Miracles on Main Street

Preface

Miracles are universal human experiences. They can happen to anyone at any time, and often do. As you read these miracle stories in the words of the people who experienced them, you will find often that the person's age, religious beliefs, physical condition or appearance, gender or sexual orientation, ethnicity, marital or economic status are not clear. *It doesn't matter.* We *all* can fall victim to danger, ill health, broken hearts, or lack of money. We *all* want to feel safe and loved. We *all* need to be recognized and respected for ourselves. And we *all* can experience miracles. As you read these stories, you can know that this could happen to you, no matter who you are.

In the course of my years of work as a writer, I have interviewed many people. In doing so, I have always been struck by the strong desire—the need, even—that people have to talk, to have someone really listen to them. But in writing this book, I have had to look much harder and dig much deeper than ever before. We all are anxious to tell of our pain, our failures, our anger, and our despair, but when asked about our miracles, we stare blankly and say, *What miracles?* When they are recounted for us, we shrug and say, "Oh, that was just a lucky coincidence," or "So the sun shines every once in a while. So what?" But we never stop talking, thinking, and worrying about all the things we think of as terrible in life, whether real or imagined.

So many miracles go by unnoticed and unappreciated every day. This book is my attempt to help change that. We need only open our eyes to their constant presence and our hearts to the profound gratitude they inspire. The more we see and accept these miracles, the more they appear in our lives and the world, and the more we can take advantage of the help and inspiration they can give us. My hope for this book is that it might help us see and appreciate that life and our world are positively brimming with miracles—wonderful, amazing, beautiful, awesome, fantastic miracles. I thank God—the Angels, the Great Spirit, the Creative Energy of the Universe—for letting miracles flow into my life and for sending me all the other stories of miracles in this book. May they flow out into the world to inspire and multiply. May we all wake up to the *ordinary* miracles ("the miracles on Main Street" of the title) happening to us and around us every day.

We have been looking for
the burning bush, the parting of the sea,
the bellowing voice from heaven.
Instead we should be looking at
the ordinary day-to-day events in our lives
for evidence of the miraculous.

—M. Scott Peck, *The Road Less Traveled*

This is a book about miracles. It's a collection of stories about people who have experienced events which they feel warrant that label. But first let's talk about the label itself. Just what are miracles, anyway? Do they require some spectacular special effects or feats that defy the laws of nature as we know them? Do they happen once in a century, a decade, or a lifetime? Do they have to be approved and certified by some governing board of miracles? Do they only happen to very special people who are somehow deemed worthy of them? I once believed all of these things, and much more, about miracles. In this way of thinking, the phrase "ordinary miracles" would be an oxymoron, a contradiction in terms. Miracles would be very rare, special events that are completely inexplicable in ordinary or even scientific terms. In other words, they almost *never* happen, and *I* certainly wouldn't be likely to ever see one if I live to be a hundred.

But I don't think of miracles in that way any longer. I see them everywhere, I hear about them all the time, I feel them happening to me day after day.

**Miracles are simply the natural process
by which the goodness of the universe finds
its way to each of us.**

When we begin seeing, feeling, and allowing miracles into our lives, we realize that their power was there all along— helping us, guiding us, leading us where we needed to go.

They're like road signs, rescue vehicles, and shelters along the pathways of life. Sometimes they intervene to stop events from happening, other times they save us from ourselves. Occasionally, they pop up out of nowhere and suddenly change *everything*.

While miracles are truly common occurrences, they are not easy to describe accurately. They involve things like a feeling that pulls us in a certain direction or a sense that now we are sure of something we didn't understand before. They can be spectacular, but are usually more subtle, speaking softly to each of us individually. It's difficult to put miracles into words that really grasp and express their effects on us. No matter how spine-tingling an experience may be for the person having it, it can always be dismissed by others. If you don't look for, don't believe in, and don't want to see miracles, you won't. If you look to disprove them, you will always be able to find "evidence" that they are "merely good luck" or "coincidental" phenomena. We are always free to choose how we will see and experience everything in life. But if we choose to look for miracles, we *will* find them. If we suspend our doubts and fears, and become open to seeing miracles, they *will* reveal themselves to us. If we open our eyes and our hearts, miracles *will* become a part of our daily lives.

Miracles arise
from a miraculous state of mind,
or a state of miracle-readiness.

—*A Course in Miracles,* Text, page 6

There is a way to become open to seeing miracles at work all around us and in our own lives. Judeo-Christian tradition calls it *faith*; Buddhists call it *detachment*; *A Course in Miracles*® calls it *miracle-readiness*. It creates both inner and outer healing; it infuses situations and relationships with love and joy; it overcomes everything and moves all kinds of mountains. It's not a magic potion or gadget that you can buy on the home shopping channel; it's not a get-rich or get-well-quick plan of action. It is, quite simply,

a state of mind.

There is tremendous power in this state of mind. When we trust someone else's abilities, they perform better. When we trust ourselves, the outer circumstances of our lives seem to run more smoothly. When we trust a spiritual power greater than ourselves—a power or energy that wants us to succeed, that is willing and able to help us transcend difficulties and overcome obstacles, and that knows what is good for us better than we do—*miracles happen*. When we let go of our human desire for control, and instead become aware, open, accepting, nonresistant, nonjudgmental, and filled with gratitude, allowing ourselves and our lives to be led wherever they need to go, when we keep our minds in the right place . . . miracles happen.

We don't *make* miracles happen in our lives, we *let* them happen. We get out of their way and allow them to occur naturally. We do this by letting go of some of our assumptions and rigid beliefs, by accepting some mystery and being open to receiving some truly wonderful surprises. We keep our minds and hearts full of faith, detachment, and miracle-readiness. We trust God or Allah or the Angels or the Great Spirit or our Higher Power or the Creative Energy of the Universe, or whatever we choose to call it, to create the best possible outcome for us in any given situation.

*What we seek we shall find;
what we flee from flees from us;
and hence the high caution that,
since we are sure of having what we wish,
we beware to ask only for high things.*

—Ralph Waldo Emerson

P rayer, meditation, and visualization are some methods we can use to help keep our minds in this state of readiness and also to express it out into the universe. They exercise our human desire to make conscious contact with a power or energy that is greater than ourselves. We use them to open our minds to the presence of spirit, to send out our gratitude and love, and probably most often, to ask for help. We call out in our need and fear and doubt. We ask to be guided, rescued, and to have the circumstances of our lives and the lives of others changed in some way. We pray for health, love, prosperity, peace, and even for greater faith, detachment, and miracle-readiness. We offer our own comfort or happiness in sacrifice for another's. We beg for forgiveness for and freedom from our human flaws. And when we do this with sincerity and humility, we are always answered, one way or another.

Thought and belief
combine into a power surge
that can literally move mountains.

—*A Course in Miracles*, Text, page 31

I believe that we humans indeed have the power to move mountains, but that we don't exercise this power nearly as often as we could. The power of our minds, our beliefs, our positive attitudes and viewpoints, lies dormant while we exercise our fears and doubts to no end. We worry, fret, stress, and agonize—as if that will ever make anything better. We replay over and over again in our minds all of the things we fear will happen instead of focusing on the positive possibilities. We think our problem only can be resolved in one specific way, and if that doesn't happen, it'll be the end of the world. We waste our time and energy fighting and resisting whatever life sends our way, instead of trusting, hoping, believing in the essential goodness and ultimate balance of the universe.

When we suspend our doubts and let go of our fears, we allow the positive energy of the universe, the will of God, or whatever you want to call it, to be done. But that's harder than it sounds, and that's why we need help. We need a storehouse of experiences to look at and say, "If *that* can happen, so can *this*." We need to believe in miracles in order to allow them into our lives, and seeing them happen—or reading about them—can give us this belief. Sharing these stories can give us something positive to focus on, to turn our thoughts away from what we are afraid of and toward the wonderful possibilities that we don't dare to believe in. If we see one mountain that has been moved, it can give us the strength to believe it can happen again—and that belief can allow it to happen.

The reason why birds can fly
and we can't
is simply that they have perfect faith,
for to have faith
is to have wings.

—James M. Barrie

One of my favorite miracle stories came from a movie I once saw about Mother Teresa. She and her nuns were supposed to deliver food and medical supplies and care to an area where gunfire made it impossible to enter. The Red Cross representatives argued that it would be foolish to get the supplies delivered to them if they could not go into the area where they were needed. The food would spoil and there was no place to store the medical supplies. But Mother Teresa dismissed their arguments with a wave of her hand. "There's going to be a cease-fire on Sunday," she stated, as a matter of fact. The Red Cross workers said there was no indication of such a cease-fire, and they couldn't assume anything of the kind. "No," said Mother Teresa, "you don't understand. We prayed to the Blessed Virgin. There's going to be a cease-fire on Sunday. So we have to get the supplies here and plan for that." She was absolutely *certain* that her prayers would be answered; there was not a trace of doubt in her view whatsoever. As far as she was concerned, it was already true, it was a *fact*. The others all thought it was completely ridiculous to believe there would be a cease-fire, and that Mother Teresa's faith was groundless and foolish, but they got the supplies to her. And, indeed, there was a sudden, unexpected cease-fire on the following Sunday. Mother Teresa and her nuns delivered the food and medical care needed, and brought out several children to be rescued from the war-torn area. When they had finished their work, the gunfire resumed.

I like to think about this story whenever my own belief in

the possibility for good is tested. Whenever I feel a great need for anything—money, health, a situation or problem resolved—I ask for the kind of pure faith that Mother Teresa showed, the faith that truly does move mountains. I try to remember all the times my prayers and meditations have manifested into reality, all the stories I've heard of others having their prayers answered, all the people who have been helped by the prayers, meditations, visualizations, and good intentions of others. I fill my mind with these stories to assuage my logical (and fearful and doubtful) brain with such precedents.

❦ ❦ ❦

Fifteen years ago,
when I graduated from medical school,
I was certain that there were no miracles.
Today I am certain that
miracles abound.

—M. Scott Peck, *The Road Less Traveled*

As I have grown older, I have developed a storehouse of memories of times when I prayed, meditated, visualized, kept my mind focused on the positive possibilities, and held onto my belief in the best possible outcome—and it happened. Sometimes I didn't get what I thought I wanted, but I got something much better. Sometimes a problem of mine was being resolved behind the scenes, without my knowledge. Often it took a long time for me to realize that my request had indeed been answered flawlessly. I have personally seen and experienced miracles, and so I believe more and more in their possibility in all kinds of situations and places. I remember other people's answered prayers and manifested faith and use those stories to help me maintain my strong belief in the power of good to come to me and fulfill my needs. Over the years, I have become stronger and stronger in using prayer, meditation, and visualization to help me survive, work through, and overcome all kinds of problems, setbacks, and obstacles.

I have now lived long enough to build up my own storehouse of stories that help me to grasp and maintain faith, detachment, and miracle-readiness whenever I need it most. It is a wonderful gift that comes with time passed and life lived consciously. A collection of examples offers us a basis upon which to build continually greater faith, hope, and trust in the goodness that is available to us all. A child believes he can learn to balance a bicycle because he's seen others do it;

a student expects to graduate through levels of knowledge and expertise, following in the footsteps of mentors.

Maybe these stories can awaken us to seeing miracles that we didn't know were happening all around us, and help us to see more opportunities for them in our own lives. Maybe they can inspire us all to allow just a few more miracles into this world, where they are so desperately needed.

Miracles

love

FRIENDSHIP

Honesty

trust

JOY

peace

COURAGE

CrEaTiViTy

kindness

c o n t e n t m e n t

COMPASSION

forgiveness

Sometimes

we have to make

s p a c e

for a miracle to flow into.

We have to let go of
old beliefs, situations, or relationships
to let new ones
take their place.

Miracles in the news . . .

A childless couple who wanted a baby very much were finally able to adopt one privately. They bonded with the infant and loved it as if it were their own. Then, suddenly, the birth father was awarded custody through some fluke in the contract or law, and they were forced to give up the child. Their story was broadcast in the local television news as a warning about the kinds of things that can go wrong in private adoptions. Two different women saw the newscast and were touched by the couple's story, their abundant love, and their wish and ability to care for a child. One woman was at the beginning of an unwanted pregnancy and the other was nearing the end of hers. They each contacted the couple through the television station, and the couple ended up adopting both babies.

*There is no
order of difficulty
in miracles.*

—*A Course in Miracles*, Text, page 1

"We were moving across the Midwest, heading for a job and friends in another state. Everything we owned was packed into our small car and a rented trailer. The weather looked bad, a snowstorm starting, so we waited a while for it to let up. But it didn't, so we finally decided to just go and hoped that maybe we'd travel away from it. We felt that we had to leave that day because the lease was up on our old apartment and the rent was paid on our new one, several hundred miles away. Looking back, we see that we could have stayed with friends and left one day later, but at the time we felt we had to go.

"If we hadn't waited we might have stayed in front of the storm, but instead it seemed to travel along with us, worsening as day turned to night. The heavy snowfall and fierce wind left no visibility at all, and we kept going for fear that stopping would only make us invisible targets for the traffic on the highway. There were so many other vehicles (mostly semi trucks) on the road, we couldn't believe it. *Who were all these people and why were they out in this weather?* We wondered. They kept appearing out of nowhere, up ahead of us or suddenly roaring past us on the side—little rows of yellow and red lights attached to nothing we could see. If we pulled over to the side of the road, we'd be buried in snow within minutes. So we kept moving, feeling our way blindly, like an airplane flying through a thick white cloud. There was nothing in front of us, behind us, above or below us, or on either side—nothing but the blinding white darkness. It was an eerie feeling. We made slow progress like this for hours.

"Suddenly, we hit a patch of ice and the car went spinning, jackknifing around and around with the trailer. Everything went into slow motion. My mind said, *We're in an accident. We're going to die. This is what it feels like to die.* I felt fine. I wasn't in pain, I wasn't afraid, I wasn't . . . anything. I was just careening through this white cloud, calmly waiting to get hit by a truck. But we didn't. Suddenly, there seemed to be no other vehicles on the road. We spun around and around, jerked by the movement of the trailer, but it was all very slow and silent and . . . *gentle.* We were flying through this white cloud, had absolutely no control over what was happening, and just sort of sat there experiencing it, letting it happen. The word *surrender* kept going through my mind. It seemed to last a long while, but yet time didn't seem to pass at all.

"When the car stopped moving, we looked at each other and said calmly, 'Are you all right?' more for reassurance that we had both experienced the same thing than actually fearing that either of us had been harmed—we *knew* we hadn't been. We both marveled at what had happened and the fact that we hadn't been hit by another car or truck—the one thing we'd been fearing on the whole trip. We laughed because we weren't sure if we'd ended up facing the right direction on the highway. We took our chances and got moving again, and made it—in the right direction—to a truck stop.

"As we sat there drinking strong hot coffee, we listened to the truckers talk about the heavy traffic and tell stories of violent accidents, of motorists stranded without snowplows or police cars or ambulances able to reach them, of not being able to see them before it was too late to avoid a collision. What had happened to us didn't seem possible. It didn't fit in with all the other stories. It began to seem like a dream, a moment suspended out of time and physical reality, when we just *existed*, and instantly realized that wherever we went, whatever we did, whatever happened to us—we would be all right. All fear was gone. All worry or expectation that something terrible might happen had disappeared. The truckers couldn't believe what had happened to us—they joked that we must have been drinking or hallucinating. The waitress said we must have had an angel in the car with us.

"We got back on the road and made slow steady progress to our destination. When our trip was almost over, the storm had subsided and we began seeing more snowplows and rescue vehicles. Flares warned us of an upcoming accident site. Flagged down by a policeman in a bright orange coat, we stopped to make way for a screaming ambulance. We saw three people taken away, and then a tow truck slowly pulled from the ditch a small car attached to a rental trailer."

Miracles are a kind of exchange;
They bring more love
to both the giver and the receiver.

—*A Course in Miracles*, Text, page 3

"It was a very busy time for me at work and I was putting in overtime every night and weekend. I was trying to manage to do everything else I needed to do early in the morning and late at night. I remember it as a time of constantly rushing around in a daze. My son's birthday cake had been ordered and I needed to pick it up on my half-hour lunch break in order to get it home in time for his birthday party that evening. I was worried about having enough time to go and get it from the bakery, get back to work in time, and leave work early enough to make it home before the party. I needed to get cash to pay for the cake. I left home at the crack of dawn to stop off at an automatic teller machine.

"The cash machine was in a small lobby at a branch bank. It was so early in the morning that the bank was closed and there was no one around anywhere. In my hurry, I hardly noticed. Fumbling with the card and struggling to remember my PIN number, I ignored the sound of the door opening and the footsteps behind me. I had to get the cash, I had to get to work, I had things to do, I had to keep moving. Just as the machine beeped at me and pushed my card back out with no cash, a young man moved up close to me from behind and mumbled 'Give me your money.' Still thinking of all my own problems—Had I put in my number wrong? Didn't I have enough money in my account to make the withdrawal? How would I pick up the birthday cake without any money?—and the urgent rush I was in, I turned to him, exasperated. He had a knife pointed at me.

"Stunned, I just stood there staring at him for a moment. Then I felt something inside me just cave in. I waved my card at him, gesturing toward the machine. 'It won't *give* me any money,' I said. I held open my empty wallet. 'See? I don't have any money either.' Suddenly giving in to my exhaustion and frustration, I went into a big spiel about how it was my son's birthday and I needed to get his cake and I didn't have any money and I was so tired and on and on. 'Now what am I going to do?' I cried. He backed off a step, with a surprised look on his face, and then said, 'I know how it is.' 'Yeah,' I said sighing, 'I guess you do.' We talked about how tough things were, about how impossible it all seemed sometimes, about feeling like giving up on everything. He put his hands—and the knife—in his pockets and shook his head in sympathy, 'Lady, you're as bad off as me.' He told me that he had a baby son himself. We talked about what we both wanted for our children—a better, easier, happier life than ours had been. We talked like that for a few minutes, shrugging our shoulders and saying things like 'What can you do?' and then I said, 'Well, I have to get to work or I'll lose my job.' He wished me good luck and left.

"When I told the story at work, everyone encouraged me to call the police and report the mugging. The bank had it all on videotape, but I had to tell the whole story and describe the man to the police. He was so young, I kept saying, and although he was bigger than me and obviously very strong, he really didn't scare me at all after the initial surprise of seeing the knife. They told me that I was just lucky, that people get hurt and even killed at automatic teller machines every day. Seeing the incident through their eyes, I suddenly felt that my life had been in danger.

"On my lunch break, I realized that I still hadn't gotten the money I needed. I looked at my receipt from that morning. It said "This machine out of service for withdrawals at this time." I went to a different cash machine, and my card worked perfectly. But when I got to the bakery, they reminded me that I had prepaid the cake when I ordered it. I had been so rushed that I had forgotten. I hadn't needed to go to the cash machine that morning at all!

"Everyone said it had been a miracle that I had not been hurt or even robbed in the mugging, but I started thinking that maybe the real miracle was that I had been there at all and had looked at that young man for a few minutes and talked to him like a human being, without fear or anger or repulsion. We'd just talked, like two ordinary people whose problems weren't all that different. Maybe nobody ever did that with him. Maybe it saved my life. Maybe it saved his."

*Knowledge and experience
do not necessarily
speak the same language.*

—Benjamin Hoff, *The Tao of Pooh*

"My father is a charmed person. Luck follows him wherever he goes. He recently won the lottery, and he has also won many trips: to Rome, the Bahamas, San Francisco, and other places. When I was ten years old—Dad would have been forty-one—he ended up having his first coronary bypass. We were walking to church on Sunday and he was short of breath. The next day he called the hospital to set up an appointment, which usually takes two to three weeks. But they had had a cancellation for that day just minutes before he called. He went in, they did a full physical, and then told him he was not leaving the hospital. Fifteen percent of the population are born with only two arteries going into the heart instead of three, and Dad was in this group. Both arteries were almost completely blocked. Had he waited another day, he was told, he would have had his first and final heart attack. His life was saved by getting an appointment that very day.

"The second time there was an angel on his shoulder was a few days before his fifty-fifth birthday. Dad and his new wife had not been in Florida for a year yet, and were still finding their way around. They had not yet chosen a family physician. My father has psoriasis, which requires a lot of medication, and he needed to see a doctor to get a prescription filled, so he called his insurance company for a referral. The doctor he was assigned was one of the few in his plan that specialize in psoriasis, and he also happens to be one of the state's foremost cardiologists. Dad made the appointment on Wednesday, for three weeks hence. He and my stepmother were out for a walk later that day, and Dad became breathless again. She suggested that he mention it to the doctor when he went in for his medication refill later in the month. When they got home from their walk, there was a message from the doctor's office that there was a cancellation for that Friday—in two days. Dad went in for his prescription, mentioned his breathlessness, and made an appointment for the following Monday for further tests. Very shortly they found that once again both of Dad's arteries were blocked—completely this time! The only one still functioning was the one they put in when I was ten years old. Once again Dad was told that had he waited any longer, he would have had a heart attack. They operated within the hour, the blockage was so extreme. Dad pulled through marvelously, just like the first time, and is walking five miles a day now. He and my stepmother have also just won a three-day cruise to the Florida Keys! How's that for 'luck'? I think my dad must have done something really great in another life."

Miracles

hope

FAITH

Caring

healing

GRATITUDE

acceptance

COMMUNICATION

InSpIrAtIoN

confidence

l a n g u a g e

INTUITION

change

growth

ETHICS

Miracles in the news . . .

A young man working on a farm got his arm caught in the machinery he was working on. Before he could be set free, the arm was completely severed from his body. Another young man who was working with him ran to the nearest gas station, called for an ambulance, and packed the severed limb in a cooler filled with ice. Doctors were able to surgically reattach the arm, and after several months of physical therapy the young man regained almost complete use of his arm.

There is a natural ebb and flow to life.

There are no peaks without valleys.

Miracles come
when it's time for them to come . . .
as long as we're not standing in their way.

*It is certain
because
it is impossible.*

—Tertullian's Rule of Faith

"I was a deacon at a church and I started a Caregivers Program for AIDS ministry. We volunteered to go in and help people do their grocery shopping, shovel their sidewalks, clean their houses—that kind of thing.

"We saw people getting sicker and sicker and we couldn't do enough for them to help them stay at home. At that point, there really wasn't a lot of home health care attention being given to people with AIDS, so people ended up in nursing homes. Many times, they ended up there alone, without family or friends—people kind of shied away from them because they were scared. So we saw a number of people die alone in situations and environments where they didn't fit or belong.

"Coupled with that, I had a friend who was HIV-positive and was doing quite well. He was living with my partner and me when he started to get sick. It was just going to be a temporary thing until he got his Social Security Disability benefits and could get his own apartment, but that never happened. It just felt so right to have him there and he felt so safe there that we just let it continue. But he used to always say to me, 'What are you going to do when I get really sick and you can't take care of me anymore because you both work? Please don't send me to a nursing home.' He would go with me a number of times to visit people in nursing homes who were dying of AIDS, and he didn't want that for himself.

"So I began wondering, *What am I going to do*? because I knew I couldn't quit my job because I couldn't afford that. Although he wasn't that sick at that point, I knew it would happen eventually. So we started to think, *Wouldn't it be nice to have a place in the city where people could live together and be taken care of and feel like they were still sort of at home, a place where their families would feel comfortable coming to be with them and help with their care without the responsibility of having to actually take care of them on a daily basis?* So I used to sit in my office at the church and look out my window and think, *How am I going to do this?*

"I visited Grace House. Although they had a very different start than we did, I liked what they had done and decided to follow their program. I got a lot of help from their director, and advice about what to do and not do. I took a grant-writing course and started writing grant proposals and sending them to anyone I could think of. About three months after the first one that I sent out, I got a response from the McKnight Foundation that said they would give us $50,000 capital money if we could match it. So it was like a blessing and a curse—to have all that money sitting there but not be able to use it.

"Around that same time, I got a call from the woman who owned this house. She said she had heard that I was looking to start a place for people with AIDS, and that she had a perfect house for me. Every time I saw a house for sale that I thought would be perfect, I would get all excited and then I wouldn't be able to do anything about it, because I didn't have the money. So I said to this woman, 'You know, I'm really burned out with that and I really don't want to look anymore until I have the money. It's too hard to keep looking and not be able to get the place.' I was sitting in my office looking out the window, talking on the phone, and I was noticing a woman walking around in her backyard talking on a cellular phone. And I thought, *Isn't that funny? She's on the phone, I'm on the phone.* . . . The woman I was talking to said, 'Why don't you just come over for coffee?' and I said 'Well, where are you?' and she said, 'Across the alley.' I looked out the window, and I said. 'Are you outside?' and she replied 'Yes,' and I told her that I had sat in this office many times looking out my window at her house and the one next door and thinking that one of those houses would probably be perfect. So I went over and as soon as I stepped inside, I *knew* that this was the house we needed to have.

"She didn't want to put the house on the market because

she was very particular about who would be in this house. But she still really wanted to sell the house, so she was trying to be patient and accommodating with my situation, but it was getting more and more difficult. We went through about five months of this, and in that time she had five different offers for the house. Each time something happened and the sale fell through. She would call me to say she had an offer and I'd say that I didn't have the money and she should go ahead and take the offer. And then she'd call me back and say that it had fallen through. Finally, on the fourth time, I said to her, 'You know, I hate to say this but I don't think you're going to sell your house until we have the money. If God wants us in that house, that's what's going to happen.'

"The fifth and last time, another offer was made. This party had heard that we were trying to get this house and we couldn't come up with the money, and so they decided that they were going to try to get this house. She called to say that she had to take their offer, that she couldn't wait any longer, and I replied that it was okay because it must not have been meant for us to be there. She asked me to come over and meet the people who wanted to buy the house. And I did, and I discovered that I had known of them through past experience with my work. I told her that I thought these people didn't really have the money. And that's exactly the way it turned out—they didn't have anything.

"The next day, I got a call from a man who said that he knew of me and what I was trying to do and that the McKnight Foundation had $50,000 for me if I could match it, and that he represented an anonymous donor who wanted to offer me $50,000. I ignored this, not thinking it was really true. But I checked this person out with some other people I knew in the community and they said they had heard of him and he was legitimate. So I called him back and asked him what I needed to do for this $50,000 and he asked me to write a grant request and get it to him by the next day. So I did.

"At this time, my friend with AIDS who was living with us had gotten quite sick with cardiomyopathy, and the doctors were saying he only had six months to live. We were really struggling with that, trying to figure out what we were going to do. He had decided that he wanted to go home to visit his family in another state for the weekend. On Friday night, his sister came to pick him up and we were saying a tearful good - bye. My partner answered the telephone upstairs and called me to get on the phone. I said I was busy, could she please take a message. She said, 'No, I really think you need to get the phone.' And I said that I was *really* busy and would she *please* take a message, and this time she said, 'GET THE PHONE!' Well, whenever she tells me something three times, I usually know that it needs to be done. So I picked up the phone and this man said, 'I'm on my way over with $50,000.'

"This house cost $109,000 and we needed to add three bathrooms. So we immediately needed about $125,000 and we had $100,000. So I went to my board and I said that we'd taken some real faith steps and they had worked out and we needed to do one more. We needed to go ahead and sign the purchase agreement on this house and believe that we're going to get the other money that we needed. So we did that and we set the closing date three months into the future in hopes of somehow coming up with the rest of the money. But the night before the closing, we still didn't have it. Grants were not being reviewed until July and August, and this was in June. So the night before the closing, one of the board members and I just started calling people and asking them for loans of $1,000 each. We told them that we didn't know exactly when we could pay them back, but we promised to pay them back with 7 percent interest. We made about 60 phone calls that night and raised $40,000.

"On my way out the door the next morning to go to the closing, the phone rang. I was going to let it ring, because we were going to be late for the closing, but my sick friend who had been with me through all of this said, 'I'll go get the car, and you answer it.' So I answered the phone and it was General Mills saying my grant had been approved and they had a check for $25,000 ready for me. We stopped by there on our way to the closing. We were late to the closing, but we had that extra $25,000.

"In every one of those events, we had done everything we could do and then had to sit back and let God do whatever was supposed to be done, and every time we did that, something would happen. So we got this house, had the remodeling done, and were ready to have an open house. But we didn't have any furniture. We had just a few thousand dollars left, enough to pay staff for about three months. We weren't really ready to open the house to residents, but we decided to go ahead with the open house. I called a consignment shop and asked to borrow furniture just for the weekend so the house would look like somebody lived there. We had this big open house planned, with the mayor cutting the ribbon, and we had invited about 400 people, because so many people had been supportive of us and we really wanted to celebrate and show them the house.

"So I sent two guys over to the consignment shop to pick out furniture and bring it over here and set it up. And it looked beautiful. I sat in here the night before the open house and thought, *How can we get this furniture? It looks so good and it needs to be here; it's just perfect here.* And the thought came to me that perhaps people would buy it for us at the open house. So I went around putting price tags on everything. At the open house, people would ask what the price tags were for and I'd say, 'If you could donate $300, we could keep that chair.' Every piece of furniture was purchased that day. We didn't have to return anything to the shop—plus we got enough extra donations so that we could buy the things that we still needed, like dishes and other such items.

"The week following the open house, the man representing the anonymous donor came back. I think that the actual donor had been at the open house, but I still don't know who it is and I signed an agreement that I wouldn't try to find out. The representative came back and said, 'I'm so impressed with what you've been able to do, by your faith and your letting God do this, that the donor wants to give you another $30,000. With that additional money we were able to open the house to its first residents; the date was Thanksgiving Day 1993. And here we are.''

✿ ✿ ✿

*The real voyage of discovery
consists not in seeking
new landscapes
but in having
new eyes.*

—Marcel Proust

"Five years after my first divorce, when I was forty-three, I married a man whom I loved at the time and grew to love even more. I understood his personality, which to me means his way of engaging other people and tasks. But he'd had a very abusive background—his father was alcoholic and physically, emotionally, and mentally abusive to his mother and to him. At one point his father had even held a gun to my husband's head. This background was never really fully reconciled within him. He really had quite a bit of hatred, which softened over the two years of my marriage to him, but there were, I believe, some genetic things that were passed on down from father to son. He became physically and emotionally abusive to me shortly after we were married.

"He was on sleep medication because he could never sleep at night and would toss and turn repeatedly and moan and never even be aware he was doing this. He took Prozac for a while, but he didn't like it. They tried him on Lithium and that didn't seem to do anything. He went into a kind of a paranoid event when we were on our honeymoon in Hawaii. I felt that it was due to stress. He would put such importance on these events—they were like escapes for him and they took on tremendous importance. If every detail wasn't perfect, it stressed him out to the max. On this particular occasion, it went even beyond that; he was not doing well. We were walking around the Polynesian Cultural Center and I suggested that we were both experiencing jetlag and why didn't we just go back to the hotel and resume this activity another day. Suddenly, he grabbed my hand

and said, 'I'm fine and don't call the police.' It was a nightmare. He was screaming my name in the middle of the Polynesian Cultural Center. It was a very difficult day.

"When we got back to the hotel room, he was really in an agitated state and he wound up pushing me up against the wall and choking me. So I grabbed the travelers' checks, quickly got out of the hotel room and took another room, and made arrangements to go back home the next day. He did the same. On the flight back, he was in tears. He was crying and was very distraught, sobbing that he did not want to lose me, that he loved me and he didn't want the marriage to end. And so the marriage continued for another fourteen or fifteen months.

"There were two more choking incidents after that, and also a lot of mental and emotional abuse in between those times. It was during the third choking incident that I finally said 'That's it,' and I pressed charges and got a restraining order. And he was really furious. He was also very clever and he convinced both our attorneys that he loved me very much and that he didn't want this divorce, he wanted to work things out and all of that. But I was pretty adamant, so then he decided we could go ahead and draw up all the divorce papers, but he would go for counseling. It could be a therapist of my choice, but he wanted me to go too. If after six months the counseling didn't work, then the divorce papers could just go through, they'd be all written up. So I agreed to that. I believed the attorneys—they both felt he was sincere and wanted this marriage to work. In retrospect, I don't believe that at all. I believe he didn't want to lose me, but it had more to do with a narcissistic kind of thing than it had to do with any real caring for me as a person. I believed that he wouldn't dare try any more physical abuse, but the emotional abuse was still present. And so I just decided that enough is enough and I told him I would not accept this abusive behavior any longer.

"He was not in treatment. He did not take any responsibility for his problems. Much of this was blamed on me. A lot of what he would say about me, I could see as truth, but there was also a great deal of mind twisting going on. So finally I thought, *No, this is just not going to work.* I think there were a lot of brain chemistry issues there, an awful lot. I believe that he is a good person, and really he wants to be loved, and he feels extremely lonely and he feels extremely depressed much of the time. But he just goes off and he's not able to sustain healthy behavior because of this brain chemistry he has.

"We finally broke up, and he called me a few months later. I knew he'd been drinking—that was part of his pattern, too; he had a lot of addictive behaviors, but none bad enough to land him in treatment for any of them. He was impulsive with money, he drank too much (but his body chemistry was such that he could really drink a lot without ever getting into trouble), and sexually he was impulsive. I think he has a high need to release much of his stress through sexual activity. So many of those addictive type of behaviors were present, and when he called me a few months later I was real firm, and I said, 'Don't call me. This is over. It's been over for a long time now and we both know it, so don't call me anymore.' I left my phone off the hook and got a number of voice-mail messages from him. I contacted the police and they did what they call a Warn and Release. There was a hang-up on my phone that day, but I don't think he's tried to call me again since then. He's an attorney, and he's not going to chance losing that identity and ability to earn income.

"The marriage legally lasted two years, and after I left him and the divorce was in the process of being finalized, I felt a log of rage. I felt a lot of rage about the decision that I had made and how I was treated and the risks I had taken, feeling like the rug was just pulled out from underneath me. I couldn't stand it. I couldn't stand all that intense anger. I couldn't stand what it was doing to me, and I knew that the only way out for me was going to be through forgiveness. I was still in the midst of the divorce process with him, and because he was an attorney, he was able to keep the abuse going in the legal arena by dragging out the court proceedings and doing all kinds of little things that kept me continuously on edge. I knew it was really important for me to regain some clarity and stability, to begin a forgiveness process.

"I really needed help at that early stage, so one evening before I went to bed I asked if I could experience what it was like to live with this man's body chemistry—which I knew from observation and from direct experience with him was a very difficult body chemistry. He would talk about his willpower and how that was the only way that he was able to get through some difficult situations and just to *be normal*, to act normally.

So I asked if I could somehow in the night, in my sleep or whatever, be allowed to know what it was like to walk in this man's shoes and kind of experience what it was like to be him.

"When I awoke the next morning, I knew that I was feeling just a fraction of what it was like to be this man. It was awful. I felt a real scrambled kind of feeling and it didn't feel at peace at all. It felt like you'd have to take a lot of willpower to concentrate on what you want to do and to project any kind of focused approach to life. It was very difficult. I imagine it's very difficult for him. I think that he has to act a lot, he has to act as if he's okay 95 percent of the time. And that has to be a tremendous burden and pressure. I think at times the pressure is so great in trying to maintain that kind of focus and to *do life* as everybody else apparently seems to do it, that that's what causes him to explode or get nasty or mean or whatever. Upon waking that morning I could feel all of this, and I knew it was just a small fraction of what he felt—for some reason I had that knowledge—and it didn't last very long. I thought, 'Oh my God, that poor man. How does he live at all?' And then it just kind of went away. Thank God, because I sure didn't want it! I did not want to feel that way.

"After that, I could understand the willpower it took for him to live every day, almost every minute, just the power of concentration it took. He was an extremely bright man, and maybe his gift was this gift of willpower that enabled him to keep himself as much in control as he was able to do. After experiencing that little bit, that fraction of his body chemistry, I kind of marveled at what he was able to do with his life professionally and trying to keep it on an even personal keel, and it was easier for me to begin the forgiveness process. It still took three years after that point to complete, but it was a good jumpstart, and it took away the rage that I was feeling towards him and it replaced that with compassion.

"This experience gave me an appreciation for how difficult it is to live with abnormal body chemistry. You have more of a compassion for people when you see them in their totality and not just what they present to you on the surface as their personality. That was really a very wonderful gift that I received as a result of this disastrous marriage. All the dreams that I'd had at that point in my life had been shattered, and that *gift of compassion* was very important to receive."

Miracles

pleasant scents

DELICIOUS FOOD

Good Service

cleanliness

WINNING

losing graciously

PAYING BACK A DEBT

HaViNg A dEbT rEpAiD

working in a garden

supporting your family

cooking a wonderful dish

finding a parking space

comforting someone

TEACHING SOMETHING

helping someone

BEING HELPED

Miracles are teaching devices
for demonstrating
it is as blessed to give
as to receive.

—*A Course in Miracles*, Text, page 4

Miracles in the news . . .

A woman who happened to be on an airplane that was hijacked by terrorists was shot and left for dead on the tarmac. They had already killed four other passengers. Eventually, all of the terrorists and all the remaining passengers on board the plane were killed in the explosion of the terrorists' bomb. Five hours after she had been shot, when the ordeal was over, rescue workers retrieved this woman's body and discovered she was still alive. Fifty-nine people had been killed, and she was the only survivor. She recovered from her injuries and now gives inspirational lectures on overcoming the effects of trauma and physical disabilities.

If you are open
to new possibilities
in your life

then that alone

will give you access
to those possibilities

—readiness is all.

—Deepak Chopra

"I began my first year at college with a specific agenda in mind. I was going to devote all my attention and time to the theater. I was planning on majoring in theater arts and had made the resolution that my extracurricular time was to be solely devoted to auditioning for shows, being in shows, doing tech for shows, and getting involved in the theater world in general. I knew that my decision to just do theater was the right choice, but when I went to the beginning-of-the-year concert that the college a cappella singing groups gave, I wished that I had enough time to be in one of them too.

"A short time after this concert one of my friends from across the hall wanted me to accompany her to her audition for the singing group she most wanted to get into. They were acclaimed to be the best group on campus, and she was nervous. She asked me to go along for moral support and also for company, as we would be walking at night. We were both getting used to the idea of safety in numbers. I didn't really want to go but I thought I should get used to doing this for friends, considering I went to school in one of the worst cities now—crime was suddenly a constant concern for us all. So I went.

"When I arrived, I sat at the side and tried not to look conspicuous or get in my friend's way. One of the group members asked me who I was and if I sang and whether I would be auditioning for any of the singing groups. I told him I was only there to accompany my friend and planned on devoting myself to theater. He said that many of the group's members were into theater and managed to do both. He said it wouldn't take up all of my time and it would be fun. He asked me about my theater experience, and I told him I had played Golda in *Fiddler on the Roof*. He told me that Tevye was a role he'd always wanted to play and talked me into singing a duet from the show with him, 'just for fun.' We sang 'Do You Love Me,' and I couldn't help acting the part instead of just singing the words. It *was* fun.

"I had mixed feelings about whether I even wanted to get into the group, although they seemed like great people the more I got to know them. I did not want to get sidetracked from my real goal of being in the theater—that was why I had come to this college. But when the night came, I waited anxiously to be 'tapped,' and as I watched my friend from across the hall get tapped and run off with another group, I knew I really wanted to get in. When the knock on my door finally came, well after midnight, I was thrilled.

"I quickly made some wonderful friendships and I've had a great experience just being part of a singing group. I've been to many places in the country on tour with the group that I probably wouldn't have gone to otherwise, and the performing is fun. I'm also doing a lot more singing than I thought I would ever get a chance to do again, even in the theater. But the best part about all this is that I met a wonderful man in the group and we fell in love. If I did not go to school in such a dangerous city, I would have never have gone to the audition with my friend or been in the group or met him. The other members of my singing group still like me to tell this story to prospective members. I like to think of it whenever I don't feel like doing something I should do or have to do. Who knows where it might lead?"

Coincidence

. . . A man goes to buy a certain kind of
lottery
ticket
and the clerk mistakenly
punches up the wrong kind.
But the man decides to buy it anyway,
plus one of the ones he really meant to buy.
The one he was sold by mistake
turns out to be a $100,000 winner.

. . . A police records clerk is off sick one day
and his replacement mistakenly
gives a lawyer access to
the wrong prisoner's records.
In these records, the lawyer discovers
evidence that completely

clears the names of eight prisoners
who have already served
four to fifteen years in prison
for crimes they didn't commit.

Coincidences, flukes, luck?
Or maybe . . .
miracles.

❧ ❧ ❧

Here's what you do:
You keep working, and you watch for

coincidence

to come strolling your way.

Watch carefully,
for it always comes in disguise.

—Richard Bach, *Running from Safety*

"It happened on a Friday night, after a long hard week when my coworker had been on vacation and I'd consequently had twice as much work to do as usual. My daughter had been ill with a rare virus, and I had just found out that someone else had been given a raise identical to mine and was making exactly the same hourly rate as I was for a very different and unequal job. I was feeling tired, undervalued at work, and worried about my family. We had recently sold our second car to pay a bill, and I had driven myself to work for a change, since my husband and daughter had nowhere they needed to go that day with her at home sick. I thought I'd take the route home that my husband liked to take when he drove me instead of the side streets I usually took. I felt like flying along the open highway by myself.

"I got into the car and drove through the parking lot in the opposite direction than the way I usually went. The car felt a little strange, making a weird noise and riding bumpy and lopsided. I couldn't believe I had a flat tire—I'd never had one before in my life. I thought there was something about newer tires that prevented that from happening except in extreme circumstances. My car had been sitting in the mall parking lot for nine hours since I had used it to run some errands before work. It had been perfectly fine then. But there was no denying that there was something wrong, so I circled the block and headed back to the spot where the car had been parked. I remembered my coworker telling me that Mall

Security would help you with car trouble as long as you were parked in a designated employee parking spot.

"I had absolutely no money to spend on getting help or repairs, and my husband had no transportation to come and help me. Back in the store, I called Security. They showed up, said they couldn't do anything, and recommended a certain gas station in the neighborhood. I asked how much that would cost me and they said they didn't know, but another woman standing nearby said probably twenty-five dollars or so. I said, 'No, forget it. I'm not spending money on this.' Security left, and another woman who also worked in the store went back outside with me and said she'd changed a tire on her own car once and would try to help me. Luckily, we owned the same make of cars and she was familiar with the tools. She got the car off the ground a little, but unfortunately, neither of us could muster the sheer strength to turn the bolts on the tire.

"I was starting to get a little angry—first, about getting the flat tire at all, and second, about being a woman and thereby dependent on others for things like this and forced to resign ourselves to paying money for our lack of relative physical strength. I went back into the store and asked a young man who worked there if he'd help. He wasn't sure how my spare worked, but consulting the manual, we figured it out. He changed the tire in five minutes without so much as breaking into a sweat. He said not to drive too fast on the spare and to be careful about sharp turns. I thanked him and he shrugged and said it was nothing. I drove home, slowly and carefully, on the side streets instead of the highway.

"While I had never really panicked about what had happened, it had been annoying and had robbed me of my flight down the highway that I'd thought might clear my mind and make me feel more relaxed. Arriving home an hour later than usual, I kicked off my shoes and flopped in front of the television. On the local news, they were in the middle of a story about someone driving on the highway about an hour earlier who'd had some sort of seizure, went crashing through two lanes of traffic, across an exit ramp, and hit a pedestrian before crashing into a wall. Several cars were involved in the accident, two people were dead and several injured. I shuddered as I realized that if I had left work and gone straight to the highway, I could have been right in the middle of that accident. I would have been in exactly the wrong place at the wrong time. If my husband had driven me, we would have been there together.

"I'll never know what would have happened if I hadn't gotten that flat tire, but I do know that the possibility was clearly there for a very different outcome for me. It's changed the way I see things, the way I think that everything happens for a reason and is all interrelated even if we can't see it. Even a lousy thing like a flat tire can be a miracle in disguise. My daughter's illness, my situation at work ... who knows what might come of *anything*? You have to accept *whatever* comes your way, because you just never know."

Miracles

cities

FARMS

Houses

airplanes

SPACESHIPS

radio

CAMERAS

TeLeViSiOn

computers

t e l e p h o n e s

FAX MACHINES

respirators

antibiotics

VITAMINS

shoes

Be of good courage, all is before you,
and time passed in the difficult
is never lost.
What is required of us is that we
love the difficult
and learn to deal with it.
In the difficult
are the friendly forces,
that hands that work on us.

—Rainer Maria Rilke

"My children were eight and eleven and I was a newly single parent, so I was under a great deal of stress. I had entered the workforce about one year previous to my divorce, so I was also fairly new to the world of work.

On one particular evening, I was exhausted, absolutely exhausted I was lying in bed on my back, feeling very hopeless and wanting not to own these problems for a while. I just laid there very still, feeling tense and helpless. Although I would typically feel tense at night, I would sleep, but it wasn't a very restful kind of sleep. So on this evening, I was feeling exhausted, I was disgusted, I was feeling hopeless. I just did not want these problems, I didn't want to own them. So I asked not to have these feelings for the night. I promised that I would claim them in the morning, I made a point of saying that—that I would claim them again in the morning, but *just for tonight, please take them away.* I had been raised Catholic and although I wasn't a practicing Catholic at the time, I did my brief meditation to the Virgin Mother, as I tend to do when I'm under a lot of stress. I don't know why, but when I really feel I need help, I just tend to turn my mind to her rather than any of the other Saints or a Higher Power or God.

"The next thing I knew it was morning and I felt each cell in my body waking up. It was like I had been in a state of suspension of some sort—almost like a coma or death or something. I just knew I had been in a state of restfulness unlike anything I had encountered previously in my life, or have encountered since. I knew that not one muscle had twitched, not one eyebrow had been raised; there was no furrow in my forehead; there had been no dreams, no nothing. It was such a really wonderful experience—I wish I could experience it again, but I have a feeling that you can only ask for these things once in a while. You need to keep ownership of your problems and develop strength to work with them.

"As I began to feel myself awaken, I remembered what my request had been and I felt that it had been granted. Gradually, of course, I could feel my problems return to me. I was reclaiming what I had said I would reclaim, and I think that's where I could really feel the difference—I was *so* at peace, and then gradually coming to the realization that *yes, this is morning and I am a single parent and I do have these problems that require my attention and some action on my part and a change of attitude.*

"But I felt like *I had been heard.* I don't know if I felt that anything was really easier after that. I know I have to take ownership; I know that I am the one who has to resolve my problems. I can pray for direction, I can pray for strength and so forth, but I have to take some action on my own part, too; I have to strengthen my abilities and my skills to meet the demands of life. But for that one night, it was just so nice to feel that I was heard and I know that there was support out there for me and I am not alone."

Love
is intimately related
with health.

—Larry Dossey, *Healing Words*

Miracles in the news . . .

A small boy was in a coma from which his doctors did not expect him to recover. His family stayed with him twenty-four hours a day, particularly his mother. She sat by his side, talking to him, reading to him, telling him stories and things that were happening in the family, singing him songs. The nurses and others told her that he couldn't hear her and she shouldn't spend so much time trying to communicate with him. They worried about her not accepting the futility of his condition and letting him go. But much to their surprise, he eventually did come out of the coma. And when he did, he knew all the stories his mother had been telling him and all the songs she had been singing to him.

What
deep
inner
beliefs
do you hold

that
stop
miracles
from coming to you?

❦ ❦ ❦

What you ask for you receive.
But this refers to
the prayer of the heart,
not the words you use in praying.

—*A Course in Miracles*, Manual for Teachers,
page 53

"I was all packed. Many times in that month I had imagined what my destination would look like. But what would I feel while there? Until now I had been boastfully successful in doing what came naturally—taking charge. No longer the competent manager I once was, I reveled in my ability to restrain all of my wild imaginings impatiently waiting to burst. To relieve the frustrated energy, I released endless torrents of busy-ness. After all, making preparations to miss work was twice the work!

"At least I knew why I was going. Undressed, the skinny legs, bony knees, and tiny feet always caught me looking at them in the mirror curiously, as if I did not recognize them. Granted, they did look different than they had even two years ago! Surely, they would fit better on a child's body. Above the counter, the tingling fingers grappled with the thin handle of my toothbrush trying hard to stay closed, round and tight. Pain pressured to lightning speed raced from knuckles to elbows as I brushed. My knees locked in pain and my head spun heavily as I bent to spit into the sink.

"The exhaustion. Joint stiffness. Tongue too thick to speak clearly anymore. The labored breathing. Slowed reflexes. Muscle spasms. Recurrent sprains and strains. The headache that never leaves. Difficulty swallowing, recuperating from common viruses, standing, walking and climbing stairs. Inability to think clearly. Increasing need for rest. Pain always on the move even when I am not. Every day, every night, every moment. *Neuropathy* is its name. I've been told that I was born with it. Only now as it makes itself known by ravaging my body, disrupting my life, I must learn to live with it.

"But at last, I was ready for bed. Even my last comfort holdout, sleep, had not been spared. That night as in the previous few years, it was a grand struggle to lure sleep fully into this body, still so foreign to me. In spurts sleep arrives, slight and restless, its healing effects hardly evident anymore upon waking.

"2:00 A.M. Something shoved me out of bed and fear suddenly surged through me. My usual hand tremors were mild compared to the shivers that began splitting my thoughts and filling my soul. Another recent invader, clumsiness, kept my body busy running into the wall in the dark. Balance, too, was no longer a given as I fought to gain control by standing in place. The floor slid from under me. *Where am I going? Who's there? Who dared to knife through my emotional umbilical cord? My dam is breaking and I've been too depleted to learn to swim! Please! Who or whatever you are, save me from drowning in my own mess!*

"Hope? What is this about Hope? I've buried hope deep inside. How could I fathom going through with this trip if I allow myself raised hopes? I could get carried away by just a little hope! To even bother considering that this sick, tired, old body could start to match the youthful facade I let other people see is absurd—*possible breakthrough drug* or not! And what about long-term effects? Modern medicine's endless list of experimental drugs and their horrific after-effects came to the rescue, halting the Hope topic in takeoff.

"I breathed. It was clearly illogical to have expectations, especially high ones. In fact, it was downright dangerous for my impressionably weak body and mourning mind. Put into perspective, this is the first drug to even be studied for use on my so-far-untreatable chronic degenerative condition. Reason prevailed: *I am fortunate to be able to participate in such research, and there are so many worse conditions I could have!*

"Staying still is scary. Use it or lose it. Contemplating paralysis, I moved. Diversion doing something I love: reading. On automatic pilot, I picked up a local weekly newspaper. Immediately, I knew I had already read it from front to back. Well almost. I never read the classifieds. Prompted by the still settling nauseous motions of fear, anger, and hope braiding tightly in my head and belly, I opened the paper up to a page called 'Eligibles.'

"Admittedly, I'd been seriously lonely since being diagnosed. Although a hereditary condition, no one else in my family has so far been afflicted with its insidious symptoms. At a convention I saw over 200 people with the disease, but the impression it left most deeply on me was the startling fact that I was one of only two conferees not in a wheelchair and able to walk minus a cane or other orthotic device. I was terrified at what I saw—clawed fingers and toes, deformed arms and legs, people walking with the gait of drunken marionettes—and shrunk from absorbing too much, cowering as if the symptoms I observed were contagious.

"Head lolling as my innards' screams started to soften, I was abruptly roused, as if by someone shaking me, to the realization that I was looking at something in particular in this part of the classified section of the paper. I recognized that I was reading the same few lines over and over again. To my eyes, the words appeared thickly bolded and in enormous typeset, as if they were the only words on the page. In reality, they were positioned in the middle of a sea of innumerable other ads crowded together in tiny print! I had been staring at these words for I don't know how long.

"Adjusting my eyes from this force-focus required enormous effort. Mind fog had become a frequent and unwelcome visitor, stealing my powers of concentration. When I managed to see and understand it, I was pleased with what the ad said. Its soft, down-to-earth, unassuming tone touched me, soothed me.

"Then suddenly, I jumped to attention as if to a military command. Instantly, I became a fully equipped soldier well versed in her mission and sat down at my computer. Effortlessly, my fingers set out to type: *Since this is the first ad I've ever responded to, I'd like to respond with the first ad I've ever written.* Studying carefully the format of the ad I had zeroed in on, I typed up my own! The result was actually a reinforcement of what the other ad said. For example, 'likes to laugh' on his ad became 'loves to laugh' in my response.

"Pure and simple, my ad wrote itself. I recall no exertion in its creation at all. By the time I finished typing the lines, I was filled with the distinct impression that someone else had been using my fingers to compose them. None of my thoughts or feelings at that point seemed emptied or put to use. Yet I felt faint, all energy spent. I crashed on my living room couch.

"At 6:00 A.M. I awoke to the sunrise beacon of grayish light shining brightly off the screen of my computer. Usually so conscientious about turning everything off, I realized it was still on, the ad I so unconsciously written now a moon pulling me magnetically toward it as if I were a destined tide. Peering into its blazing surface, I felt myself obliged to fulfill some unexplained expectation it evidently had of me. Without hesitation, I printed the ad. Then I changed fonts and printed another copy. The two pages were left abandoned, attached to each other in my printer, as I left my PC to shower and make breakfast.

"Bathed and fed, this uncanny feeling took me by the hand and led me once again. I was directed to take what I had written out of my printer, but not to toss it into the trash. Only at this time did I turn off my computer for the first time all night. The next thing I knew, I was scrambling to find a page in the newspaper which would tell me how to send an ad to someone else! Totally unaware as to how it was accomplished, the envelope was properly addressed with my ad snugly inside. As if duly following orders again, I dressed and drove to a nearby store to get some cash since the ad required a couple of dollars to process. My ride arrived at 8:00 A.M. sharp. Since it was Sunday, there was no rush in sending out mail. But on the way to the Mayo Clinic, I had the driver stop at a mailbox.

"That night, I regretted sending the ad. Questions starting bursting forth: *Why? How? What made me do such a thing?* I felt so vulnerable! A shallow sense of security came from knowing that my phone number was not offered in my ad, nor my name: only my mailing address and initials. Even so, just think of it! Succumbing to such foolishness! *What could I have been thinking?* And how could I play with such serious work ahead of me—the I.V. in my arm, the nurses all around, the ever more important questions and other probings the doctors required of me as a dutiful guinea pig?!

"My self-esteem was really the most obvious casualty in all of this medical invasion. It had been broken to the point of being afraid to hope for a better future for myself in the arena of personal relationships. But then how could it have been *me* who responded to an ad in the Personals? Denial embraced me and I returned the hug gratefully. Just like my stubborn insistence that this ailing body couldn't possibly be attached to me—and thus I was able to present it proudly as an object to be poked and probed for the sake of research—detachment saved me from thoughts regarding relationships. This Jekyll-and-Hyde mentality allowed me to fluctuate between my emotional and physical worlds, separating them not only from each other, but from my own identity entirely.

"This split flourished early on, simplifying the complexity my life was becoming, helping me to deal with each new difficulty I was forced to face. It was born out of my intense terror of crying—and never being able to stop—over my predicament. It allowed me to fool the outside world into believing that I was at peace with myself and pushed away unwanted attention. A most transparent disguise to everyone but me; a lie that kept me from feeling.

"A month passed. I'd survived two visits for treatments administered at the big clinic with little discomfort. I'd reluctantly learned that comfort is relative and not something I'm able to truly attain physically anyway, so I didn't sweat much from the trials and tribulations of medical testing.

"I did confide, though, in my mother. I confessed the whole 'Eligibles' ad incident to her sympathetic, nonjudgmental ear. Supportive as always, she advised me to go easy on myself. I was also riding on waves of relief that my ad had *not* prompted a response, letting me off one hook to focus on another: the grueling anticipation of medical results.

"Thirty days from the day I sent the ad and left for the Mayo Clinic, I received a piece of mail with only my initials on it. It turned out to be responsible for my meeting the most wonderful human being I will ever know, my true soulmate. And after only three weeks, I—who had previously been in relationships that lasted five years and longer, and had *never* wanted to marry—knew without a trace of doubt that I wanted to be with this man forever. Our compatibility and complementary features fit as if fated. So maybe it was not completely by chance that I was the *only* person who responded to his ad and that it was the *only* time he'd ever placed a Personals ad. Perhaps even the friend who had coaxed him into it with a bet had been part of some greater force none of us had been aware of.

"The Mayo Clinic results I received later proved to be disappointing, the new breakthrough drug useless for my physical condition. But my grief and disappointment have transformed into an utter joy I never allowed myself to imagine I would ever be blessed with! Even more valuable, I am able to share my pain openly with a sincere, caring man and to be there for him when he needs to share his woes with someone. Mysterious, patient, and yes, even *hopeful* was the gentle guiding force that visited me in my most painful hour to remind me of and to push me to work for reclaiming my most precious commodity: love.

"Although my handwriting will continue to disintegrate, and my ability to accomplish tasks requiring any adept manual dexterity or bodily strength are on the decline, *I feel brilliantly alive, fully nourished, amazingly strong, and blushingly healthy in my heart!* Even in pain, I can also feel love. On the first anniversary of our being together, my love proposed to me. As I plan our upcoming wedding, I ponder the lesson that my invisible guide brought to me: **Health of the spirit is much more meaningful and necessary for a good life than physical health.**"

*The invariable mark of wisdom
is to see the miraculous
in the common.*

—Ralph Waldo Emerson

Miracles

art

MUSIC

Bridges

roads

TRAINS

schools

CHURCHES

CoMmUnItY cEnTeRs

mammograms

h e a r i n g   a i d s

EYEGLASSES

hospitals

medicine

FOOD

Sometimes we have to wait for miracles. They don't happen exactly *when* or *how* we wish they would. We do all the things we think we should, keep our minds focused and positive and open to receiving, and still nothing changes. But if we don't give up hope, if we accept that the resolution to our problem or situation may not be what we thought it should, eventually it will be resolved. Sometimes it almost seems as if the universe is waiting for a specific date on the calendar, and then suddenly many things start falling into place simultaneously. Or several things may take a long time to happen, like a slow-motion domino effect.

We need to remain patient, positive, hopeful, open and alert to the miracles that are coming to us. Sometimes we don't realize what the miracles are until later. Sometimes a whole set of circumstances or events have to take place in preparation for what we thought we wanted to begin with. And sometimes we just don't know why, but the miracles make us wait a bit. They show up when we least expect them to, in surprising ways. That's why we need to let go and trust them. They'll come . . . in their own perfect time and way. And when they do, they're well worth any exercise in patience we've had to endure.

Maybe learning patience is even a part of the miracle.

Every day
there are miracles
for those who are aware
through faith
and believe.

—Tom Brown, Jr., *The Vision*

"We were finally going to be able to leave a place where we were unhappy living and didn't want our young children to go to school. We had moved at least ten times in our ten years of marriage, and there was a lot of resistance from our relatives to this move. But they were at least part of the reason we wanted to go. We felt compelled to go someplace where no one knew us or any of our relations, to really find out who *we* were and how we wanted to live and raise our children. We wanted to be a family all by ourselves. It seemed very important for us to do so.

"My husband had been offered a new job in another state, and the company was going to pay for our move. But after two trips to look for housing, we still hadn't found anyplace to live, and time was running short. I prayed and prayed, imagining exactly what we needed—a house to rent, with two bedrooms, an office for my work, a fenced-in yard for our dog, and in a nice neighborhood where we could all feel comfortable. Without a dime to spare, my husband took one more trip alone to find a place for us to live—even something temporary, we thought, and then we could find something else when we were there. But again he found nothing.

"On his last day in town, as a desperate last resort, he paid for one of those housing search services that everyone said were a waste of money and only took ads out of the newspaper anyway. The very first address on the list they gave him turned out to be a lovely house, perfect for us in every way. The rent was affordable, the neighborhood was great. He thought it couldn't be true—it was too perfect. It was as if we had special-ordered exactly what we needed and wanted! But there was one catch—the owner had been trying to sell the house, and had only decided to get renters in for a while to help cover his costs until it sold. We took the house with the understanding that it would be shown for sale and if it did sell, we would be given six weeks' notice to leave. We loved the house, but we thought at least we'd be able to search for something else once we were living there.

"The house sold almost immediately. We were panic-stricken. New in a town where we didn't know anybody, leaving behind bad feelings with people who'd made it clear that they thought we were being both selfish and foolish, we started worrying and doubting ourselves. Days of anxiety turned into weeks. We had as much trouble finding another place to live as we'd had originally.

"Again I prayed and prayed. I made a conscious effort to accept this turn of events, to be positive, to believe that good would come to us in the end. I kept thinking that if this perfect house could have been given to us in the first place, then this new problem could also be resolved for us. I turned it over to God and asked to be able to stay in the house or to be given another one that was just as great for our needs. I kept looking for another house and trying to remain open to whatever would come my way as an answer to my prayers. We enjoyed and took good care of the house we were in, and even planted flowers in the yard, not knowing whether we would still be there to see them blossom.

"One day the soon-to-be new owner came to see us. She turned out to be a lovely woman who was not even interested in living in the house right away. She was happy to have renters in it to take care of it for her until she was ready to retire and move back to town. We signed a new lease that day and settled into that perfect house, where we lived without another thought of moving for *nine* wonderful years."

❦ ❦ ❦

Perhaps miracles simply obey laws
that we humans
generally and currently
do not understand.

—M. Scott Peck, *The Road Less Traveled*

"I have often felt in my life that something or someone wants me alive. I have had numerous near-misses when something terrible might have happened to me but didn't. Several of these incidents involved cars.

"I think I was only about ten years old when the first one happened. It was outside New York City, in Yonkers, a very hilly city. I was coming from the library. My parents' car was parked across the street and they were waiting for me. So I came out of the library and I stood on the curb, and there were cars parked there. I looked up and down the street from between the parked cars—very carefully, several times. And then I stepped out. Suddenly, a car sped up the hill and came so close to hitting me that when it stopped, my hand was on the front bumper!

"I had looked carefully, had not seen nor heard anything coming, and neither had my parents. It was a completely sudden thing. I was not harmed at all, other than feeling a little bit shaky. It scared me, and I think it scared the driver a lot, too, and of course my parents were both really shook up. And even at that young age, I remember thinking that this was a little bit more than just luck. My hand was planted so firmly on the bumper of that car that even then I felt it was divine intervention that kept me from being hit by that car.

"Another time, a few years ago, I was the driver. It was late in the day and the sun hadn't set, so it was at that eye level—

where it just hits you in the eyes and blinds you. And for some reason, I suddenly put my foot on the brake. I wasn't sure why I was doing that. And then in just a moment, two or three seconds later, this child ran in front of my vehicle. I really felt that *I* had not put my foot on that pedal, but was directed to and it just went there. I don't remember thinking before I moved my foot; suddenly it was just there on the brake. All I remember is feeling blinded by the sun, braking the car, and then this child darted out in front of me. If I hadn't braked when I did, I know I would have hit him. The kid and his father were fine; they appreciated my ability to stop when I did. But I didn't see any ability in that, because *I* didn't do anything. It was just like suddenly the car braked and I thought, *I really didn't do that.* But I also didn't hit that child because of it.

"The third time, I was delivering magazines to a home that was high up on a cliff overlooking the Minnesota River Valley. It was icy, so when I went to pull the car back down the driveway, it slid onto the edge of the embankment. I was hanging on the edge there and I felt that if I were to go over, I'd go down into a bunch of trees, down this steep embankment. I'm not sure how far I would have gone down. I assume the trees would have stopped the car at some point. I felt I would have been hurt—maybe not killed, but it was a very scary experience. I had to have one foot on the brake and one foot on the gas pedal and work them both to get the car going backwards, because one more inch forward and I would have gone down and been mangled in the trees.

"I got the car inched backwards and backed it up and turned it around, so that I could take an alternate road down the hill. And when I turned the car around, the very first thing in my vision was this statue of Saint Francis of Assisi that I had never seen before, even though I had been to this house many times. Either I had never seen it or it had never registered in my memory before, but on that day it was right there and the message that came to me was: *You're not doing this life alone; there are forces helping you, whether you think so or not.*

"All these incidents are examples of what I have always felt as some kind of force that somehow wants me alive. I could have been hurt or even killed several times, but I have always felt the presence of . . . *something* taking care of me. It saved me on these three occasions, and probably a lot more times that I don't even know about. These are just the ones I remember that made me believe that there is someone or something out there that wants me to keep on living."

Miracles

air

TREES

Water

flowers

MOUNTAINS

summer

AUTUMN

WiNtEr

spring

o c e a n s

SUNSHINE

butterflies

lightning

BIRDS

snow

RAIN

All miracles are healings of some sort.

They cure negative circumstances,
change the course of events,
heal old wounds,
close old doors
and open new ones.
They unearth deep secrets
and shine brightly
into dark corners.
They cuddle and comfort,
unshackle and push us forward.
They spin us around
and set us down on new roads,
sometimes dizzy and confused.
They ferret out the roots
of our discontent
and cure their causes.
They free us of our own mistakes,
and give us

always

one more chance.

"I went into business for myself because I wanted to be independent, to be my own boss, to do work I wanted to do instead of what somebody else wanted. I wanted to use what I had learned to be my strengths and abilities without interference from a lot of other people. I took a huge risk and plunged in.

"Much to my surprise, I succeeded beyond my wildest dreams. It was as if I was being told that I had made the right decision, that I was being helped to succeed because I was doing the right thing. I felt so *affirmed*. My first job came only one month after I'd left the security of working for someone else, and after a few months of working hard at it for almost no money, it finally paid off. After that, it was one job after another and more money that I had ever imagined I would earn.

"Since I had started out with some old debts, it took a while before I actually felt like I was making some good money. Then, I started choosing what to spend it on. I wanted certain things for myself and my family, but not anything you could call luxurious. I wanted to live in a nice house in a nice neighborhood, but what you call *nice* is relative, isn't it? I wanted to stay in the city instead of moving out to the sterile suburbs, so of course I got less for my money in terms of newer, more luxurious material things. But I didn't care about that. I wanted to live someplace real. The house I chose needed a little work, and that took another chunk of money after the down payment and closing costs.

"I spent money on my children's education and on experiences rather than things. I wanted to travel, to learn things, to broaden my knowledge and understanding of the world. In other words, aside from the house and a modest car, I didn't have a lot of stuff to show for my money. But I was living the life I had always wanted for myself and my family. That, to me, was what prosperity was all about. I fully expected the income to continue and even increase over the coming years.

"For the first two years, I made extremely good money; the third year I made very good money; the fourth year I made good money, and the fifth year I bottomed out. I had to take a job to make up some of my loss. At this point, I was still positive and hopeful. I figured I'd just take this little job to tide me over until the next big break, the next great contract. I worked two full-time jobs between my job and my self-employment, and all I had time for was work. But I still loved it and fully believed that it would soon turn back to the way it had been. I was perfectly willing to work harder for a while and even to work for someone else, knowing it was only temporary.

"For a whole year, I worked harder than I have ever worked in my life. I had complete faith and hope that my hard work would pay off eventually, and I would get back on a better financial footing. But I was falling into debt, borrowing from one pocket to pay another. I exercised every inner strength I had, asked for extensions and made arrangements to pay some things over time. Every time a creditor agreed to a new arrangement, I felt affirmed again, as if I was being helped to stay afloat, rewarded for my perseverance and hard work. I knew that I had always been terribly independent and needed to learn to ask for help and accept it sometimes. I felt like I was learning and growing even from this temporary hardship. I tried to make the best of it.

"For a whole year, I lived on faith and hope. I truly believed that new work was coming to me, that the people who kept promising me contracts and money would come through if I just held on long enough. But, to make a long story short, they didn't. The contracts didn't come, the money didn't come, and even old sources of income I had come to rely on suddenly dried up. My job—one that paid less than I had earned in about fifteen years—became my only source of income. For the first time, I started doubting my ability, my decision to do this thing, and everything I had believed in with such faith and hope.

"By this time, I was behind on so many debts, it was no longer possible to hold off one while paying another and then pay that one and let the other one slide and so on. I just couldn't pay my bills. It was December, winter, and Christmas was approaching. I had no money to pay my kids' college bills or to get them home for the holidays, much less to buy them gifts. I thought a lot about the life insurance policy that had been one of the things I'd finally bought when I had the money, having never had life insurance on myself before. With the money from that policy, all my debts could be paid and my family would be all right. It wasn't that I was depressed exactly. I just thought that this would be a logical solution to my problems and I didn't see any other possible solutions. I finally realized that the contracts and money I had believed in were not going to come to me. And this was real life, not that *It's A Wonderful Life* crap that was all over the TV at that time of year. People were not going to come out of the woodwork to save my butt and pay my debts for me.

"So I thought I should die. I wasn't despondent or sad or anything like that. I didn't want to die, you understand. I just thought that was what should happen. So I prayed for it. I thought about suicide, but I didn't really want to do that to my family and I didn't think I could do it anyway. The worst thing I could imagine happening was that I'd try it and not succeed. Then, besides all the financial problems, I'd be thrown in a loony bin and then where would my family be? I thought if God would just take me, everything would be all right. I knew my family would be sad and all that, but they'd get over it . . . and they'd have enough money to get out of debt and go on with their lives. I offered my life for my family's sake, because I thought that was all I had left to offer them. I even wrote up instructions for my funeral and for filing the insurance claim and disbursing the money to pay my debts, and put it in my safety deposit box.

"About this time, I heard from an old friend of mine who I hadn't seen in years. While I hadn't talked about my financial problems or my wish to die with anyone, I found it all pouring out over the phone with this person. When I had finished, a story was told to me that I had never heard before. It seemed that my friend had once been exactly where I was now.. I learned about a failed business venture, creditors calling, showing up at work and at home, harassing my friend's family. I heard about the seizure of property—boats, hunting equipment, snowmobiles, and cars. I learned about the threatened foreclosure on my friend's home. I felt sick to my stomach.

"But my friend went on. In 1979, the U.S. Congress changed a law and allowed individuals and self-employed business persons to file a Chapter 13 Bankruptcy or Wage-Earner Reorganization of Debt. My friend had been one of the first to benefit from this law. The foreclosure was halted. The creditors were ordered by the court to stop harassment tactics. The debt was consolidated and monthly payments were set up that my friend could afford. The whole thing was a huge strain on my friend's marriage and family, but they were given a second chance. The business was dissolved, there would be no chance of getting credit for a while, but by working for someone else, the monthly payments were manageable and they were able to keep their house.

"My friend gave me the name of the attorney who had 'been very sensitive' and 'understood everything' they were going through, and had helped them through the whole process. The week before Christmas, I called and made an appointment to talk with this attorney to see if he could help me. I was still prepared to die any time God saw fit to take me; I still thought that would be the best solution I could think of. But I swallowed my feelings of having failed, swallowed my pride, and asked the lawyer for help.

"In our first conversation, I could see that my friend had been right about this man. He was sensitive, understanding, and very respectful of me and the position I was in. He went over everything with me in great detail. I told him everything I had tried to do to pay my debts—borrowing against my insurance and retirement funds, applying for a home equity loan, and selling my second car. We went over everything I owned for possible cash value. Because I hadn't spent my money on luxury items, there wasn't anything to sell. We calculated my potential gain from selling my house. He told me about bankruptcy fraud and how people sometimes try to hide assets and the court catches them. I trusted his honesty and knowledge of the process. He said that bankruptcy is a good thing for some people in some circumstances; you just have to get over the word. After two hours of talking to me without any assurance that I would even file or pay him a fee, he left me with a lot of information and advised me to think about it.

"The next day I signed the paperwork and paid the filing fee. I still felt a complete failure. I still asked God to take my life if it was His will. I knew that filing would affect me for years to come. But I also knew there was nothing else to do. I finally gave in and accepted my situation and all the things I had done and not done to get there. I filed because I had no other choices left. I don't recommend that anyone ever think of this as a potential rescue or excuse to take stupid risks, and I certainly don't condone the kind of fraud that I was shocked to hear about from my lawyer, but there are times when bankruptcy is truly a Godsend. It was for me. It was a second chance, a lesson in forgiveness and starting over, in letting go of pride and accepting the help that is out there for us.

"When I threw all my credit cards into a roaring fire in my fireplace on New Year's Eve (along with the envelope containing the instructions for after my death), I felt an indescribable sense of freedom. One era in my life ended and another began. I am still self-employed and still working a full-time job; I think of both as gifts. I make my monthly payments to the trustee of the court—and all my bills—with gratitude and joy. I love living simply, without debts I can't pay. My children are getting Financial Aid and working part-time while they're in school. My family has become closer than ever, working through all of these problems together. We had our best Christmas together ever, with fewer presents and much more appreciation for everything.

"My friend told me that in the end the only real thing that matters is being together and getting through life one day at a time. Money is nothing; pride is nothing; success and failure are nothing. If, in the end, you're still standing and your loved ones are standing beside you, *you have everything.*"

❦ ❦ ❦

The prayer for forgiveness
is nothing more than a request
that you may be able to recognize
what you already have.

—*A Course in Miracles*, Text, page 45

"My maternal grandmother died when I was sixteen. I was extremely close to her and I suffered from enormous feelings of guilt regarding her death. My mother and I used to visit her regularly in the nursing home where she lived for a few months. On this particular night I didn't want to go visit her; I wanted to do something with my friends. My mom and I fought about whether or not I should go visit Gram. I finally won out and went with my friends. When I got home, Mom called to tell me Gram was in the hospital, but Mom said to wait until morning to come. Gram died before I got to see her.

"I carried this guilt for years and thought about her a lot. During my sophomore year in college, Gram came to talk with me at my apartment. It was an incredible experience! She came to tell me to be at peace with myself; that she did not blame me for wanting to be with my friends and that she loved me and knew how much I loved her. What I saw was Gram from the waist up, and the bottom of her just kind of misted out. I remember feeling so happy to see and talk to her. When she said she had to leave, I begged her to stay, but she said she had to go. I asked if she would come back again, but she said no, she couldn't. I remember grabbing onto her hand and pleading with her to stay. She looked into my eyes deeply and said, 'I love you and now I must go.' I felt the tug of her hand and at that split second I realized that if I let go she would be gone forever and if I hung on, I would be pulled with her and I would be dead. There was no doubt in my mind that this was true. I let go and have not seen Gram since.

"I have gone to her grave once. That was when I was pregnant with my first child. I cried because Gram would never know my husband and children and I asked for Gram's spirit to come back in my child. I don't know if that has happened, but I know I have Gram's love and forgiveness."

All things work together for good.

—Romans 8:28

"I had been involved with my boyfriend off and on for about two and a half years. We had just gotten back together before I left for college, and things were good but as insecure as they had always been. We were happy for the time being, and just couldn't let go of each other yet. At school, I met someone new. He was the sweetest, most interesting, romantic, intelligent, attractive man that I had ever met.

"I was supposed to go visit my old boyfriend one weekend, and I decided to make this the weekend where I would tell him about the new person in my life and see what happened. I wasn't sure which way I was going to end up going. I loved them both, but my old boyfriend and I were at a crossroads where I needed more of a commitment from him and needed to know he really loved me and wanted this relationship.

"I was getting a ride from a couple of guys in my dorm and was waiting for them to call. They had to go get the car from one of their relatives who lived half an hour away. The minutes passed and still no call. I was packing some last-minute items when I realized that I couldn't find my St. Christopher medal anywhere. I *always* wear it so that I have a safe trip, and it really unnerved me that I couldn't find it! I didn't want to go without it. I searched for it frantically, and had a sort of spooky feeling about not being able to find it.

"My new friend was waiting with me to say good-bye. I kept telling him he didn't have to wait, but he insisted on keeping me company. Time passed. I was getting tired, frustrated, and angry. *What was taking those guys so long to pick me up?* And why couldn't I find my St. Christopher medal?

"I called my old boyfriend to tell him what was going on, and realized that he was drunk. I had made him promise me that he wouldn't drink until I got there because I wanted to have some time with him to talk seriously before he partied too hard. So now I was mad at him, and told him I'd get there *sometime*. More hours passed, and the guys I was supposed to get the ride from finally called to say that they couldn't come to get me because they had been trying to get the CLUB off the car they were to borrow for the past several hours—the relative had forgotten to leave the key or they had lost it or something.

"I was very upset and depressed. I had wasted the entire evening waiting for these guys who never showed up, I was all packed for a trip I wasn't going to end up taking, my old boyfriend had lost no time in partying even before he knew I was going to be late, and I still couldn't find my St. Christopher medal! My new friend cheered me up and took me out for pizza. He was wonderful to me and we ended up having a great time.

"The next morning I slept in late. When I finally woke up and stumbled to my desk, I saw the most amazing thing. There, right in front of my eyes, was my St. Christopher medal hanging from my lamp! There was no way I could have missed seeing it the night before. That's when I realized that I just wasn't meant to go see my old boyfriend that weekend.

Everything went wrong that could have gone wrong to stop me from going. I probably would have ended up staying with him and missing out on the most wonderful relationship I have ever had. A decision I might have made was made for me. Some force had kept me from going, and I knew that what had happened was *meant* to happen."

*Ask,
and ye shall receive,
that your joy may be full.*

—John 16:24

"I was born on my maternal Grandmother's birthday. My mother had a long labor and I was born at one o'clock in the morning, so she always joked about how I'd refused to be born until Grandma's special day.

"When my own daughter was born, I delivered her several days earlier than expected. Grandma was very religious and always seemed to me to have a direct pipeline to Heaven. After my daughter was born, she told me that she had prayed for the birth to be on that day instead of on my due date. Several years earlier, my uncle—her youngest son—had died of cancer on that date. She told me that she'd asked for my baby to be born on the same day of the year so that every year she would be able to remember *both* events, and a bad day would be turned into a good day from then on. Her prayers were answered."

Miracles

gardens
DESERTS
Rivers
rocks
HEAT
cold
SURF
CoLoR
rapids
c a n y o n s
waterfalls
vegetables
fruit
ANIMALS
plants
PEOPLE

Miracles in the news . . .

A story ran in a city newspaper about a new center for homeless families, including a school for homeless children. In less than a month, thousands of dollars in cash were donated to the center, along with thousands more in merchandise. Offers for services ranging from auto repairs to tutoring poured in. Clothes, books, toys, food, and even apartments were suddenly made available to many people who'd had nothing. Various individuals and groups came forward to offer whatever was needed to make the center and school successful in helping homeless families.

*Miracles
may not always have
observable effects.*

—*A Course in Miracles*, Text, page 5

"I don't know if anyone else would call this a miracle, but I certainly do. I've been getting migraine headaches since I was a teenager. Most of the time, they're manageable with pain killers, and although I don't ever get complete relief from them, I can do most of what I need to do in my daily life. I get through them knowing that they'll last two to four days, and then they'll be over. Sometimes, though, they're a lot worse. The pain can be excruciating and not respond to any drugs or therapy, and I'll suffer from visual disturbances and vomiting as well.

I hadn't had a really bad attack, with all of the symptoms, in about two years—until about a month ago. I felt it coming on and took my prescription medication as usual. The migraine hung on for days, just sort of lurking there in the background of my life—painful, but not intolerable. I kept thinking, *Only one or two more days*, and it would be gone. But it didn't happen. After a whole week—which was longer than I had ever had a migraine before—I suddenly became violently ill. When I woke up one morning, the pain was so bad that I couldn't stop crying. No amount of medication helped at all. I began having what I call "kaleidoscope vision"—everything looked broken up into a circle of geometric shapes. Diamonds spun around before me, and I couldn't focus on anything. Closing my eyes, blinking, nothing I did made it stop. It was the most frightening thing I've ever experienced. I thought I was going blind. Between the pain and the visual disturbances, I couldn't even call work to say I wasn't going to be able to come in.

Around noon, my eyes began focusing again, and I started vomiting. That lasted an hour. Afterwards, I was mercifully able to sleep for the rest of the afternoon.

"I stayed home from work one more day, still feeling a headache, but able to nibble crackers and drink tea and nap. My vision was normal again. The next day I returned to work, feeling wrung out, headachy, and tired. I was told that I 'looked like death.' After that was the weekend, which I spent resting at home. That migraine had lasted a solid ten days.

"A week later, on Saturday afternoon, I found myself grocery shopping. I hadn't been able to do it during the week, when the shops were less crowded, the lines shorter, the parking spaces closer to the building. But I had to go out and get it done on Saturday. I found myself rather enjoying the store—leisurely roaming the aisles, letting the busy, harried impatient, and very unhappy-looking folks go on by me. Eventually, I took my turn checking out, paying, and taking my plastic cards with big numbers on them for picking up my groceries outside. I strolled out of the store and into the warm sunshine.

"In the couple of minutes it took me to walk from the building to my car—way at the far end of the crowded parking lot—my mind began a litany of the wonderful things around and inside me. I felt a surge of happiness and gratitude because I was healthy enough to not need one of those handicapped parking places right up front, that I could easily walk out to my car. I felt blissful that my body worked! I was filled with joy at the warmth and sunshine; the blue sky and white clouds and green trees and grass; the car I would drive home and the gasoline that filled its tank; the pavement under my feet; the money which had bought my groceries; the food itself; the store; my clothes; my sunglasses; the home I would drive to and my husband who would be there, cutting the grass; the fact that I didn't have a migraine at that particular moment! There was no end to the list my mind kept making of things, one after another, all the way from the store to my car. I can hardly describe what that walk was like for me. It was an epiphany. It was a clear, solid moment of pure joy and love and happiness and gratitude. It was a miracle to really, truly appreciate all the miracles in that moment. It was the sudden realization that what we take for granted as *normal* is truly *amazing* and *wonderful* and *awesome*! In that moment, nothing escaped my attention, my rejoicing, my heart's thankfulness.

"If I hadn't had that killer headache, would I ever have experienced that moment of pure joy? Would I have made a doctor's appointment to see what kinds of new medicines are available for migraines? Would I have started thinking about something I read somewhere that said headaches may be caused by trying to hold two conflicting belief systems in your mind at once? Would I have spent time every day since looking at things differently, more closely, with more respect and wonder and gratitude? Would I have appreciated all the joy that can be found in what we call *ordinary*?

"Although it was an incredible experience for me, I don't suppose anyone watching me walk from the store to my car that day could see anything unusual or miraculous going on. Unless maybe it was my slow, relaxed gait, or the little smile I couldn't keep off my face even if I had wanted to. I think it's still there."

🌱 🌱 🌱

Miracles deserve respect.

Cars, boats, airplanes, and spaceships
are miracles;
but they need to be properly
built, run and cared for,
and their effects on the rest of the world
need to be considered and addressed.

Relationships are miracles;
but we have to take responsibility
for our own part in them.

Our bodies are miracles,
but we must maintain their health and
fitness.
Our minds are miracles,
but we are responsible for their

use and development.

All miracles
require our care, our
responsibility, our
respect.
And, miraculously . . .
we're capable of giving it to them.

❦ ❦ ❦

At some point
we care with all our heart
and then we finally let go.
We give it all we have
and trust the rest
to God, to Nature, to the Universe.

—Ram Dass & Paul Gorman, *How Can*
I Help?

"My husband had a drinking problem. Actually, it had become *my* problem because I always had to make up for his drinking. I felt like a single parent, working and cooking and cleaning and doing everything for the family with no help at all. I had already been through years of convincing myself that it was okay, that it was normal to drink like he did. Then, I went through years of begging him to cut back, and believing him when he said he would. I was so tired of it all, so worn out and used up and sick of feeling angry, afraid, resentful, depressed, and unhappy.

"Finally, I just couldn't stand it anymore and I couldn't pretend it was okay. I thought and thought about what to do. I imagined all kinds of scenarios, and realized that none of them could be worse than what I was already living with. I had seen my mother waste her whole life on an alcoholic husband, and I didn't want to do the same. I didn't want my kids to grow up the way I did. After years of kidding myself and covering up for him to other people, I just gave up.

"The end finally came when my husband didn't come home from work one night. He didn't call and I called his office, but he wasn't there. In front of the children, I pretended that everything was okay and he was just working late. I fed them dinner, helped them with their homework, gave them their baths, read them stories and put them to bed. But inside, I was struggling with fear and worry alternating with rage. After the children were asleep, I called everyone I could think of, including the local hospitals and the police. The hospitals had no record of him in their emergency rooms, and the police seemed to think it was pretty funny—a wife all upset about a husband who just wasn't home yet several hours after he should have left work. I finally called the home of one of his coworkers and his wife said that he'd gone out for drinks after work and she didn't expect him home until quite late. It was already quite late, and I called the bar where I knew he'd stopped off for drinks after work before. I asked the bartender to page my husband, and he put me on hold—for a long time. I hung up and called back, asking again if my husband was there. The bartender starting yelling at me, beginning with something like, "How in the f— should I know?!" going on from there with more abusive language and ending sometime after I had slammed down the phone on him without saying another word. I sat there, shaking and crying, feeling as if I'd been attacked by this verbal violence. I heard a car door slam outside.

"My husband had been offered a ride home by the last person to leave the little party at the bar. He literally fell into the front door and passed out. I didn't want the children to find him there the next morning, so I dragged him to bed. A strange kind of calmness came over me then. I knew that something was over and something new was now going to happen. I felt something inside me change instantly, and I knew that I would be all right. I had hit the end of what I was willing to take, and suddenly, without any more anger or fear or doubt, I *knew* what I had to do.

"The next day I sat my husband down and told him calmly and quietly that I had had enough of the way things were. There were no tears and no arguments. I just said that he had a choice to make: me and the kids or booze. For the first time, I wasn't afraid anymore. I wasn't afraid of being alone—I was already alone. I knew I couldn't make him change or do anything. All I could do was decide what *I* was going to do and then be prepared to do it. It was a very simple choice and the only one he had left, I told him, and he must have seen that I really, truly meant it.

"My husband went to his first AA meeting and hasn't had a drink since that day. It has been a long, hard road, but we are making it one day at a time. I am very grateful for how well things have worked out for us, that he was ready to hear what I was saying and he did stop drinking and start working on getting healthier in lots of ways. But I also believe the real miracle was that feeling inside of me, that turning point when ·I just knew what I had to do and was completely ready to do it. If, after that, he had continued drinking or gone back to it, I would have calmly wished him well and left him. It would have been okay. *I* would have been okay. And I think that realization had a lot to do with things working out as well as they did."

🌱 🌱 🌱

Miracles are

ignored
overlooked
taken for granted
brushed off
disbelieved
and belittled.

Would you

keep coming back
to someone
who did that to you?

Things just happen in the right way,
at the right time.
At least they do
when you let them.

—Benjamin Hoff, *The Tao of Pooh*

"I graduated from the university with a B.A. in Psychology two years ago. Since then, I've been working in a bookstore. I wasn't positive of the direction I was taking with my professional interests in psychology, so I didn't fill out any applications. I figured that I'd know what I wanted when I came across it.

"A few months ago, I was at my friend Kevin's house when another mutual friend, Jeff, happened to call. We had all been to high school together. I talked with Jeff about school and the fact that we both had degrees in psychology. Kevin had told me that Jeff really liked his job, so I asked about it. It sounded interesting, so I told Jeff to let me know if there were any openings. It was only the second job that had even interested me since I'd graduated. I enjoy psychology, but have very specific ideas about what I'd like to do in the field.

"Jeff called me about an opening the day before I left for vacation, and by the time I applied, when I returned, the position had been filled. I asked them to keep my résumé on file. Three weeks later, another position became available, and they called me for an interview. (I should interrupt to say that I had been visualizing myself at this job ever since Jeff first told me about it at Kevin's. It was with a larger company, with full benefits, including the fact that they would pay 100 percent of my school tuition to go back and get my Masters degree, *plus* they offered a salary greater than I ever thought I'd make without a Masters in a psych-related field!) I went to the interview and to a second interview two days later.

Instead of trying to not jinx the position by not talking about applying for it, I told everyone about it—*everyone*! It was the only thing I could think about. I could so clearly see myself doing it. The more people I told about it, the more real and clear the visualization became for me.

"At first, they offered me a part-time position, and I accepted it, planning to continue working part time at the bookstore to make ends meet. I asked if there was a possibility of moving up to a full-time job, but the supervisor said that they did not have a high turnover, so he couldn't guarantee it. I felt calm, though, and still saw myself working there full time. The next day, after I had accepted the part-time position, someone unexpectedly resigned and they offered me the full-time job. Of course, I took it!

"I don't know if it was just that I knew what I wanted—where I'd fit in—when I saw it or if visualizing helped, or what. But whatever it was, it worked and I love my new job!"

Miracles

getting sick
GETTING WELL
Being Truthful
listening to someone
BEING LISTENED TO
smiling
CRYING
LaUgHtEr
childhood
p a r e n t h o o d
getting married
getting divorced
giving birth
BEING BORN
living
DYING

❦ ❦ ❦

Miracles occur naturally
as expressions of love.
The real miracle
is the love that inspires them.

—*A Course in Miracles*, Text, page 3

"My sister and I had never really gotten along. We grew up together, like sisters do, going through some times of seeming close and more times of fighting and competing with each other. We were different in so many ways. School and other intellectual pursuits came easily to me; she resented that. She was always so pretty and thin and people liked her; I resented that. We both had our share of successes and defeats, but we always seemed to feel the other one had things easier or better.

"We chose different colleges, hundreds of miles from each other, at least in part to escape one another. After that, we drifted even further apart, although we kept up regular visits and occasional letters and phone calls. On the surface, I guess it seemed like we got along well, but I always felt that she was tearing down my accomplishments and still competing with me. I tried to ignore it, make excuses for it, and pretend there was nothing wrong, but being around her always had a way of making me feel bad inside.

"We both married and had children, pursued careers and . . . grew up. I believed, for a while, that we had outgrown our childhood resentments and competitiveness, and had really grown close. But later on, I realized that I had been mistaken. My sister cut me off suddenly when I got my Masters degree. I don't know if that was just a coincidence or if she was jealous or what, but she just stopped speaking to me. I don't know if I did something specific that made her angry, because she never talked to me about it. She just stopped calling, writing, and visiting. When we called her to arrange for a visit on our vacation, she never returned our calls, so we went somewhere else. Our relationship simply ended, abruptly and without any apparent reason. There was no argument or anger or anything. Just silence.

"I was really confused about it for a while. I kept thinking of all kinds of things I might have done to offend her. I got angry about my children suddenly being cut off from their aunt, uncle, and cousins without a word. Whatever her resentments toward me, my sister could have given a moment's thought to my small children and their bewilderment and feeling that they must have done something wrong to make their relatives stop liking them. I started seeing our whole relationship differently. Actually, all the things I've said about our competing and resenting each other and all of that . . . I didn't really realize until after this happened. I had always thought we were close. But now I knew that I had been kidding myself.

"Except for the hurt she inflicted on my children, I was able to let go of my relationship with my sister easily and quickly. She'd never really known me, anyway. I felt that I had been nothing more to her than a cardboard cutout in her life, that she had never really recognized me as a person with a mind and feelings and viewpoint and life of my own. I had casual acquaintances who knew me better than she did. I looked back over our lifetime together and realized that it had never been what I'd believed at the time. I realized that without her in my life, there was really no particular void left except the *idea* of the way families ought to be and the *idea* of how nice it would be to have all those relatives getting along and loving and supporting each other. But the fantasy of visits and vacations and picnics and cousins growing up together . . . well, it was only a fantasy. We were all just fine without it.

"We grew older, our families grew up, and we never spoke, wrote, or saw each other for years. Then, last year, my sister had a stroke. My widowed father called me, and all the relatives met at the hospital. We waited in the hallway together to hear how she was doing and what was going to happen. We prayed and hugged and held hands. Suddenly, they came crashing out of the emergency room—my sister on a gurney, doctors and nurses flying around pushing her along with all kinds of machines and tubes and bottles and hoses and instruments. They pushed past us to the end of the corridor and into an elevator. We were told by a harried doctor that she needed emergency surgery, and her chances for survival were slim.

"Hours later, when the surgery was complete, and we had been told that my sister had made a miraculous turnaround and would be all right, her husband and our father were allowed to see her for a minute. When they came back, they were both crying. She said to tell us all that she loved us, they said. Days later, when she was getting stronger, her husband told me that she was asking for me, so I went to the hospital. My sister cried as she told of her experience in the emergency room, and yet there was this sort of blissful radiance about her as she spoke. She said that she had felt herself leave her body and float above it, watching what was going on. At first, she said, she didn't understand what all the fuss was about, why the doctors and nurses were working so frantically over her body—she was fine, she said, she *felt* fine. She let them do their work, and started looking around. She described seeing us all there in the hallway, worrying about her, and said that she was filled with an overwhelming sense of complete and unconditional love for us all.

"My sister talked for a long time that day, about life and love and how we shouldn't waste time. She said that she felt like a different person, like she had been *reborn* somehow. She said that there's this whole dimension to life that we never see and it makes everything else seem so unimportant and even stupid. She said that life is about nothing but love, this overwhelming, underlying love that's everywhere, only we don't see it or feel it most of the time. She said that she decided to go back into her body to take a second chance at living that love.

"From that day on, my sister and I have been close friends. We have never talked about the time before her stroke. It just doesn't seem to matter anymore."

If we could see
the miracle of a single flower
clearly,
our whole life would change.

—Jack Kornfield, *Buddha's Little
Instruction Book*

The Buddha taught that "life is suffering." If we accept life as painful and difficult; if we accept the pain, difficulty, disappointment, and tragedy as the rule rather than the exception; if we accept all the things we judge as "bad" as the norm . . .

then every good thing—every pleasant, happy event or situation; every healthy relationship; every beautiful, peaceful moment; every "lucky" turn of events; everything that's "not bad"—can be accepted and appreciated as a happy surprise, a wonderful gift . . .

a miracle.

Try This . . .

For just one day, try thinking of everything *you see and experience as a* Miracle.

. . . a tree . . . a rock . . .

A SMILE . . . A LAUGH . . . A TOUCH . . .

Television . . . Books . . . Words . . . Clouds . . .

leaves . . . rain . . . birds . . . weeds . . . flowers . . .

THOUGHTS . . . FEELINGS . . . IDEAS . . .

photographs . . . telephones . . .

SLEEP . . . DREAMS . . . HUGS . . . KISSES . . .

FoOd . . . WaTeR . . . ElEcTrIc LiGhT . . .

colors . . . paper . . . do. . . wheels . . .

cars . . . apples . . . dogs . . . computers . . .

clocks . . . mirrors . . . chimneys . . . stereos . . .

cherries . . . games . . . furnitures . . .

vegetables . . . umbrellas . . . children . . .

SCHOOLS . . . CLOTHING . . . SPOONS . . . GLASS . . .

mountains . . . rainbows . . . gardens . . .

TALKING . . . WRITING . . . READING . . .

being . . .

To me
*every hour of the light and dark
is a miracle,
Every cubic inch of space
is a miracle.*

—Walt Whitman, *Miracles*

If you came here looking for the answers to the mysteries of the universe, you came to the wrong place. I don't have them any more than you do. I just think we would all do well to recover our childlike sense of hope and wonder and appreciation for all the miracles that make up our world, our universe, humanity, and all of life.

Cynicism is *easy*. We can all look around, throw up our hands and say, "Ain't it awful?" Does that make it any less awful? Does it help anything at all? Hopelessness and negativity don't make us more intelligent or sophisticated; they simply make us and our lives more hopeless and negative. Hope is the truly difficult part of life. Positive faith requires an enormous amount of concentrated energy. Hope and faith are hard work, and both pay off accordingly.

Try letting yourself be *amazed* for a change. Dare to see through the eyes of a newcomer to this world. Don't let the miracles slip by, day after day. *See* them. *Appreciate* them. Be *thankful* for them. And *let* them happen. Take a chance—cynicism will always be there waiting for you, anytime you choose to go back to its illusion of safety.

What have you got to lose?

But don't listen to me; don't listen to anyone. Listen to everyone. Listen to the birds and the trees and the surf and the sand. Listen to the wind and the thunder and the rhythmic drumbeat of your own heart. Listen to the silence. That's where the miracles are . . .

e v e r y w h e r e.

Those who are

awake

live in a state of
constant amazement.

—Jack Kornfield, *Buddha's Little
Instruction Book*

I've heard this joke about positive thinking:

"I used to go in for positive thinking, but bad things kept happening, so I gave it up."

Okay, that is amusing in an ironic sort of way, but it also shows clearly just how far off the mark we often are in understanding this whole idea of "positive thinking" or seeing miracles.

A warrior had a fine stallion.
Everyone said how lucky he was to have such a
fine horse.
Maybe, he said.
One day the stallion ran off.
The people said it was unlucky.
Maybe, he said.
The next day the stallion returned
leading a string of fine ponies.
The people said it was very lucky.
Maybe, the warrior said.
Later, the warrior's son
was thrown from one of the ponies
and broke his leg.
The people said it was unlucky.
Maybe, the warrior said.
The next week the chief led a war party
against another tribe.

Many young men died
in the fighting.
**The warrior's son,
because of his broken leg,
was left behind
and so was spared.**

—Native American legend

Recently, my house was hit by lightning in a violent thunderstorm. I was awakened from my sleep in the middle of the night by a loud *boom* right outside my bedroom window, and then a *pop* and a *crack*. Through the window, I saw a bright ball of sparks fly off the roof. It was like Fourth of July fireworks right outside my window.

Fortunately, no one was injured and all the electrical damage to the house and appliances could be repaired. But the experience is one I will never forget, and my husband and I have thought a lot about what had happened and what we could learn from it. First of all, none of us or our animals was hurt. We felt a very strong sense of well-being in the midst of all this chaos. We felt that whatever happened, we would be okay. Secondly, we realized that the only damage that was done was to things we didn't really need. We were reminded that, if we had to, we could easily live without a lot of the things we were used to having. We felt a real sense of peace about it. We didn't get upset or view it as a terrible thing that had happened to us. We just shrugged our shoulders and decided that anything that wasn't covered by our insurance and we couldn't afford to replace we could do without. It had been a shocking, frightening experience, but it was soon over and we were truly just fine.

My husband and I both recognized that a few years earlier, we would *not* have responded to such an event with such serenity. We would have felt victimized; we would have been filled with anger, worry, and all kinds of negative emotions that would have lingered with us for a long time. We would have been wringing our hands over the catastrophe that had befallen us. The distress would have found its way into our bodies, manifesting in stomach pains or headaches. We would have become irritable and short-tempered, causing problems in our relationships and our work.

But now we didn't. We took what had happened in stride and got on with our lives. As soon as we'd decided that we could live without anything that had been damaged, it started looking like everything could be fixed or replaced without any trouble. We made all the phone calls we had to make, and got on with the job of cleaning up.

Surveying the damage outdoors, we saw that, besides the house itself, at least one huge tree near our house had been hit. Large splinters of fresh wood were scattered all over our yard and our neighbor's yard. A huge branch lay on the ground at our front door. Examining it, we saw that it had been dead or dying, with only a few leaves clinging on to the little bit of nourishment that was still getting through. "Nature's pruning," we called it, and chopped up the branch for firewood. Ironically, I had refused a man selling firewood door to door off the back of his truck only the day before. It was a bargain price, but I didn't think we could afford it, anyway, especially in August. I would think about getting firewood later, I thought, when the weather started turning cool. Now I didn't have to.

I accept the universe.

—Margaret Fuller

I have learned from a lifetime of personal experience with miracles that . . .

I will be all right no matter what happens,

something good can come out of anything,

and

*I can always learn something from everything
that happens.*

I didn't talk myself out of being upset about the lightning strike, or repress any feelings about it—I simply responded the way I responded. Clichés like "Every cloud has a silver lining," "Look on the bright side," and "This too shall pass" are no longer just clichés to me. They have profound meaning. I've lived long enough now to be able to shrug my shoulders and say "I've survived worse than this" about nearly anything. I have a collection of memories that serve my rational mind as proof that miracles can and do happen all the time.

❦ ❦ ❦

A miracle is never lost.
It may touch people
you have not even met
and produce undreamed of changes
in situations
of which you are not even aware.

—*A Course in Miracles*, Text, page 6

When we pray or meditate, visualize and ask for assistance, we can't help but watch for the results. Are our prayers being answered? How and how quickly are our visualizations manifesting into reality? Are we getting something we asked for or something else? Sometimes our prayers, meditations, and visualizations are having concrete effects, but we just can't see them. It's important to remember to let go and allow the answers to come in their own way and time.

Think of it this way: when the snow melts in the late winter and early spring, it reveals an earth that shows no signs of life. Soil lies smooth, unmoved by root or stem. Dead twigs and branches stand barren and brittle. But time passes, and invariably, life breaks through the soil and appears miraculously upon the dry vines. The earth bursts forth with lush, green, growing, pulsing life. Year after year we witness this miracle, and so we expect it, believe in it, have complete faith in it. When our prayers, meditations, and visualizations seem to go unheard, we can remember the still ground of late winter, throbbing just beneath the surface with the sweet buds of spring and the magnificent lush abundance of summer.

Demand not
that events should happen
as you wish,
but wish them to happen as they do,
and you will go on well.

—Epictetus, *Discourses*

Sometimes we can't quite see what's happening, but other times we do see that what we asked for is *not* coming to pass. We may pray for someone to be healed, but their disease advances; we may visualize a job, house, relationship, money, or some other specific outcome, but not get it. We may clear our minds and open up to creative inspiration, but nothing seems to come. When this happens, it's important to keep our belief in the mysterious workings of a universe we don't fully understand. It's important not to blame ourselves or to believe that we didn't get what we asked for because we don't deserve it. Nobody in the world *deserves* miracles—we are all flawed human beings. Miracles don't happen because we're *good enough* for them; they happen because that's what they do. And they're doing it all the time, without our even knowing it.

Sometimes it's the best thing for us to *not* get what we ask for or think we need. Sometimes the miracle is the answer "no" to our prayers and meditations. Our conscious mind can't see or know everything involved in many situations and relationships. When we turn our requests over to a higher form of understanding and power, we may get even better help than we asked for. Sometimes things that look like bad luck or setbacks are really the best possible outcomes in the long run. And sometimes we just have to accept that we don't know the reasons why.

It isn't always necessary to know
how the body ought to behave
for healing to occur.
One need only pray for "what's best"—
the "Thy will be done" approach.

—Larry Dossey, *Healing Words*

To be accepting and open to *all* the miracles—even the ones we would never think to ask for—some people ask for "this, or something better." Others ask only for "what's best" in any given situation. This keeps our minds from getting too stuck on one particular outcome that we want to happen. It acknowledges the reality that we don't always know what the best outcome would be. It helps us to see the good in everything that comes our way and enables us to be in a constant state of gratitude.

＊ ＊ ＊

Miracles
should inspire gratitude,
not awe.

—*A Course in Miracles*, Text, page 5

🌿 🌿 🌿

*There is nothing so natural
to the human heart
as the desire
to give thanks.*

—Matthew Fox, *Creation Spirituality*

Gratitude is a very important part of experiencing miracles. It is an awareness of their presence and work in our lives. It is an acceptance and joy in receiving the good of the universe. When you go to the trouble to give someone a gift that you know they'll find useful or will bring them happiness in some way, doesn't their sincere gratitude feel like a gift back to you? When you go out of your way to help someone out, doesn't it feel like no sacrifice at all if they truly seem to appreciate it? Don't these experiences of gratitude make you want to give again? Gratitude can help to open up the channel through which miracles can flow freely into our lives. And as soon as we start recognizing the miracles all around us, we find gratitude to be our true natural state of mind.

When our perils are past,
shall our gratitude sleep?

—George Canning

You pray in your distress
and in your need;
would that you might pray also
in the fullness of your joy
and in your days of abundance.

—Kahlil Gibran, *The Prophet*

I hope that this collection of stories has helped you to believe in miracles a little more. I hope it is now somewhat easier for you to hold on and keep believing, hoping, trusting in the goodness that pervades the universe, even when you can't see it. I hope you have begun to recognize some miracle stories in your own life and all around you, and that those stories begin to multiply as you go forward from here. I wish you what is truly best in every aspect of your life and the peace of spirit to enjoy it all.

For what has been—thanks!
For what shall be—yes!

—Dag Hammerskjöld

MIRACLE EXERCISES

Here are a few exercises for you to try that will help you open up to seeing and facilitating the miracles all around you. Practicing these exercises daily can really make a difference in your outlook and your life.

Finding "Little" Miracles

Spend a few minutes thinking of all the good, pleasant, happy, positive, abundant, fruitful, and not-"bad" things that you have seen, heard about, or experienced in the past twenty-four hours. They can be as small as having enough money to put gasoline in your car or buy a cup of coffee; not having a pain, ache, disease, or injury; sharing a moment with someone whose company you enjoy; hearing a pleasant song on the radio; seeing a pretty bird, tree, or cloud; having clothes to keep yourself warm; having hot running water to bathe in; laughing; getting work done; voting; eating; stretching; sleeping; paying bills; cooking; singing; smiling; helping; letting go of worries, fears, doubts, and anger. Make a conscious effort to look for "Miracles in the news." Ask yourself: *What good things have I seen, done, or heard about today?* Nothing is too small. Write these things down in a journal or notebook.

Focusing Energy

Relax. Let go. Breathe deeply. Feel the energy within you. Let it hum and glow throughout your entire body. When you have a good, solid feeling of this energy, focus it on some aspect of your life or your surroundings. Send your energy like a long ribbon of bright light flowing outward from you to this object or situation. Feel only love, peace, and joy emanating from you toward whatever it is. Feel the healing quality of this light connecting you and it. Feel that you are one, that the energy flowing through you is the same energy flowing through the object of your attention. You are in complete harmony with each other and the whole world. It is all the same energy. Focus on this image for a few minutes. Feel the peace and happiness it gives you. Let it fade gradually from your mind, but keep the feeling of oneness and love.

Finding Blockages

Sometimes we find certain areas of our lives to be particularly problematic for us. These areas hold some power for us that we may not even be consciously aware of. Ask yourself: *What is it in me that wants to keep this problem? What belief in me would be threatened by its resolution and disappearance from my life?* You may encounter a lot of resistance at first—of course, we say to ourselves, "I don't *want* to have these problems!" But give yourself a chance to discover an old belief or connection in your mind that prevents you from solving or letting go of these problems. Perhaps something in you associates having enough money with being greedy or evil in some way; maybe an old idea still exists within you that miracles won't happen for you until you lose weight or get more education or a better job; or maybe you feel uncomfortable claiming miracles for yourself, believing they only happen to perfect, saintly people. Finding these hidden beliefs is the first step to freeing ourselves from the ways in which they can block our acceptance and appreciation of miracles.

Release

Once we have located problem beliefs, we can lovingly let them go. They were not formed to hurt us on purpose. They are errors that we can now let go of without fear. Usually, discovering them is followed by a great feeling of relief. Then we proceed to find that letting them go intellectually is easier than stopping their effects on our thinking, our behavior, and our lives. Patiently, we can remember where they came from and that we no longer need or want them. Gently, we can take responsibility for them and choose to let them go. We can visualize writing them down and sending them off in a hot-air balloon or handing them over to God, an Angel, or whatever form of Higher Power we choose to visualize.

New Beliefs

Having cleared out an old belief that was stopping us from seeing or accepting miracles, we can now replace it with a new corresponding belief. For example, if your old belief was that you could never be happy in love and secure in money at the same time, you can now affirm that indeed you *can* have both and that in fact they go hand in hand. Each old belief will have its own appropriate new belief. Affirm these new beliefs by repeating them over and over to yourself, writing them down, and talking about them with other people. Make them real by *not* keeping them secret. They are now a part of the current you.

Imagining the Possibilities

Practice healing small problems and areas of your life by finding a blockage belief, releasing it, replacing it, and focusing your—and the whole world's—positive energy on it. It's important to start small and feel the success of letting a little miracle into your life. Believe that something will work out fine, whether it's finding a parking place or arranging a meeting. Turn it over to the miraculous energy of the universe, your idea of God or Angles or some Higher Power, and *let* it turn out well. Don't anticipate *how* it will turn out well, just get out of its way and assume that whatever happens will be perfect. Go about your normal business, believing that all will unfold as it should and accept whatever happens gratefully. Gradually, you can imagine healings in more and more difficult or significant areas of your life.

Calling Energy

Being open and receptive to miracles is important for them to be able to work in our lives. Relax, breathe deeply, and imagine yourself in some open natural place—a beach, a mountaintop, a field. Feel the energy within and all around you. Reach up to the sky and say, "I am ready to receive all the goodness of the universe." Turn in all directions and repeat this affirmation. Then repeat, "The goodness of the world flows freely to me and through me to others." Turn all around again, calling out your affirmation to all directions. Feel that you are one with all the positive energy in the world and universe.

Gratitude

Feeling and expressing thanks is an inseparable part of miracle-readiness. It is not something we do just once in a while, for specific reasons. While we can and should express our gratitude for certain things we feel we have been given, gratitude can also become a constant state of mind for us. Every day, think about things to be grateful for, however small. Feel the *feeling* of thankfulness frequently, and know its joy. Send gratitude out to your God, Allah, Angels, Saints, Great Spirit, Creative Energy of the Universe; to people, animals, and plants that share and support your life on earth. Stand in your natural place, stretch out your arms to the sky, and say toward all directions:

**"Thank you for all of your blessings—
past, present, and future."**